Sunset
Hors d'oeuvres
APPETIZERS, SPREADS & DIPS

By the Editors of
Sunset Books
and Sunset Magazine

Lane Publishing Co. • Menlo Park, California

Supervising Editor: Elizabeth Hogan
Research and Text: Lynne B. Morrall

Special Consultant: Mary Jane Swanson
                                Staff Home Economist, Sunset Magazine
Photography: Glenn Christiansen
Artwork: Patricia Kinley
Design: Cynthia Hanson

Front Cover: *Super Nachos,* recipe on page 15.
                Photograph by Glenn Christiansen.

Title Page: Cheese course from *Food and Wine
                Tasting Party,* page 78. Photograph
                by Glenn Christiansen.

Editor, Sunset Books: David E. Clark

Fifth Printing October 1979

Contents

the Hors d'oeuvre Experience   4
from preparation to presentation

Dips, Spreads, & Fondues   8
smooth & mellow or hot & spicy

Hot Appetizers   28
from the stove, the oven, or the barbecue

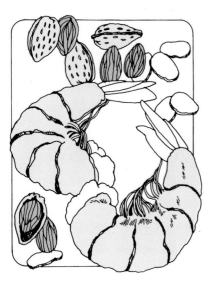

Cold Appetizers   56
cool & refreshing make-ahead hors d'oeuvres

Party Menus   68
Nothing-to-it, Wine Tasting, Ethnic Themes

Index   79

Special Features

Bagna Cauda—Serve-Yourself Italian-style Appetizer   14
Fresh Creamy Cheese   19
Nut-studded Appetizer Cheeses   22
Classic Swiss Fondue   27
When the Pastry Chef Makes Hors d'oeuvres   36
Appetizers from the Barbecue   40
Smoked Salmon from the Barbecue   44
Geometry and Sleight of Hand
     with Party Sandwiches   63
Cheese with Fruit and Vegetable Accompaniments   66
Spirited Liquid Refreshment—Hot or Cold   74

the Hors d'oeuvre Experience
from preparation to presentation

Hors d'oeuvres—miniature morsels of food—are fun to make and a delight to eat. Best of all, hors d'oeuvres are a joy to serve, for they give you, the cook, a golden opportunity to display your culinary talents.

Whether you're planning TV snacks for the family, finger foods for the cocktail hour, or a reception for 100 guests, the recipes you'll find here will be a welcome sight. With more than 200 to choose from, you can please not only yourself but also fans of your unique brand of cuisine.

The following chapters are filled with a broad selection of hors d'oeuvre recipes, from the simplest (seasoned popcorn) to the more involved (fancy canapés).

Recipes for foods served in individual portions appear in two chapters, "Hot

Party Appetizers (clockwise from upper left): Curry Dip and crisp raw carrots (page 13); Crisp-baked Artichoke Appetizers (page 41), Happy Hour Mushrooms (page 39), Hasty Hots (page 41); Spicy Cocktail Wieners (page 43); Mini-Bagels (page 36), fresh cream cheese and Smoked Salmon (page 44).

Appetizers'' and ''Cold Appetizers.''
''Dips, Spreads, and Fondues'' deals with foods presented in a different way—instead of passing them, you place these appetizers on a table so guests can serve themselves. The last chapter, ''Party Menus,'' coordinates recipes from other chapters into parties with a variety of themes.

What Shall I Serve?

By French definition an addition ''outside the main work'' of the menu, hors d'oeuvres form the light and delicate complement to the main course. Whether you plan a cocktail party or a simple Sunday afternoon gathering, your hors d'oeuvre selection should reflect the size and purpose of your party.

The occasion will influence your choice of beverage, too. At an exuberant kind of party, you would be wise to serve beer or white wine instead of red wine or other beverages that could stain if spilled in the excitement of cheering. In any case, be particularly considerate when planning the beverages you'll serve. Will any nondrinkers be invited? If so, have nonalcoholic beverages on hand.

To simplify your role and to allow for movement of the party, plan to have some appetizers to be passed, others to be left on tables for guests to serve themselves.

If you are moving on from hors d'oeuvres to dinner, a pleasant way to announce the transition is to serve your guests mugs of hot broth or a simple soup. This ''walk-around soup,'' served on the patio or in the living room, lets guests know cocktail time is over and gives the host or hostess time to make final preparations for the meal. Soup suggestions appear in the ''Nothing-to-It-Party'' feature.

Balancing the Menu

Besides seeking a good balance of hot and cold appetizers, you'll want to vary your menu in other ways. Contrasting flavors and textures always make for a more in-teresting meal or party. Consider having some crunchy hors d'oeuvres and some smooth ones, some that are spicy and rich, others that are light and refreshing.

For a large party, plan on at least one appetizer from each of the following categories: meat, fish, cheese, vegetable, and fruit. You'll want to serve a good balance of types of food for a small gathering, too, but on a smaller scale.

How Much Will I Need?

Unfortunately no hard and fast rules exist that will apply to every party. Weather seems to be a determining factor when planning how much food you'll need. People tend to eat more in cold weather, drink more in warm weather.

For foods that will be passed, expect to serve at least two of each kind of hors d'oeuvre per person. You will want to pass at least six appetizers per hour and supplement with serve-yourself foods on the tables.

For estimating beverage quantities, see ''Liquid Refreshment,'' pages 74 and 75.

Consider the Guest

Try to recall the most successful parties you've ever been to. They probably weren't the most lavish, elegant, or complicated. Nor were they the ones cast with the most sparkling guest list. Undoubtedly they were the parties where the guests and the hosts felt comfortable and relaxed . . . the ambience made the difference. Keep this in mind as you move through all the stages of your party planning and presentation.

Make your guests comfortable. Let them feel that they are an important part of the whole party scene. Set up the atmosphere of the party—a blazing fire and steamy mugs of mulled wine in winter, a festive outdoor setting and chilled bottles of white wine in summer. Such amenities waiting for the first arrivals will make them feel welcome and relaxed.

Will you be serving hot finger foods? Remember that your guests may not be feeling as cautious as they might under less festive circumstances. Warn them that something is *hot* before they take a bite. Hold off serving foods until the bacon has stopped sizzling and the cheese is no longer bubbling and steamy. Piping hot foods are a delight, but not if the results are painful.

Be cautious when serving unusual foods. People not interested in eating unconventional foods, such as escargots or chicken livers, won't appreciate finding out that that's just what they've eaten. Some people are allergic to certain foods, such as seafood, dairy products, spices, and nuts. Since these ingredients are easily camouflaged, be sure to volunteer a brief list of ingredients if a worried-looking guest asks, "What's in this?"

In the same spirit, tell guests what's in a mixed punch, particularly if it will deliver its own kind of *punch*.

The Drop-in Guest

If you are fond of inviting people in for cocktails on the spur of the moment—or if your spouse specializes in such surprises—you'll welcome the following list of suggested staples to keep in your pantry, freezer, and refrigerator for impromptu gatherings.

• canned or frozen pâté • packaged fondue • frozen bread cubes for fondue • frozen spreads • frozen prepared appetizers, ready to pop in the oven • flour and corn tortillas • peta bread • sour cream • low-fat or regular plain yogurt • cream cheese • green onions • a variety of crackers • marinated artichoke hearts • canned California green chiles • liquid hot pepper seasoning • soy sauce • canned water chestnuts • canned salmon and crab • smoked oysters • chafing dish fuel • cocktail-size paper napkins

Budgeting Your Time

Unless you work exceptionally well under pressure, make sure all the marketing and incidentals are taken care of well in advance. Prepare ahead of time as many dishes as possible. Make a list of what remains to be done the day of the party and consider how much time each item will take.

Remember that *you* are an important part of the party's atmosphere. If you feel everything is under control, you'll be relaxed and so will your guests.

Hints for Freezing Hors d'oeuvres

With most of the recipes in this book, we've included freezing information. Here, in addition, are some basic guidelines you can follow.

To store any type of hors d'oeuvre in the freezer, we suggest using a specially designed freezer wrap, such as heavy aluminum foil, heavily waxed or laminated paper, or plastic bags and containers designed especially for freezing.

• **Sandwiches and canapes.** Freeze only if they *do not* contain mayonnaise or sour cream in their fillings, for these ingredients tend to separate. Use butter or margarine, salad dressing, or cream cheese for moistness instead. Don't freeze fillings that contain pieces of crisp vegetables, hard-cooked egg whites, and tomatoes. Wrap sandwiches and canapés, individually or in small groups, in freezer wrap and freeze as long as 3 to 4 weeks.

• **Puff shells and crisp toast bases.** Freeze these separately from their fillings and from other appetizers to prevent them from gathering moisture. Wrap tightly in freezer wrap and freeze as long as 3 to 4 weeks. You may need to recrisp them in the oven before serving.

• **Stuffed olives and nuts, bacon-wrapped tidbits, or cheese rolls.** To freeze, place in single layers on metal pans. When frozen solid, package in shallow containers that hold not more than 2 or 3 layers. Separate layers with freezer wrap. Then overwrap entire container with freezer wrap and freeze as long as 2 to 4 months.

• **Dips and spreads.** Freeze those that contain cheese, ham and cold cuts, fish, avocado, and egg yolk mixtures (but *not* mayonnaise or sour cream) in plastic containers. Freeze as long as 2 to 4 months.

Dips, Spreads, & Fondues

smooth & mellow or hot & spicy

Mexican-inspired Guacamole, elegant Creamy Pâté, and Classic Swiss Fondue —these are three enticing examples of what's ahead, each representing one of the three categories of appetizer recipes on the following 18 pages.

Though many of the simpler dips in this chapter are based on sour cream and cream cheese, others feature more exotic combinations. For example, Thai Chile Sauce is a spicy mixture of green apple, chiles, and anchovy paste. More demure palates may prefer Shrimp Dip, a creamy shellfish delight punctuated with toasted slivered almonds. Nachos (pictured on the front cover) combines several simple dips and garnishes into an extravagant-looking display.

We've also included such classic dips as Blender Hollandaise and Green Goddess Dip (pictured on the opposite page). Among dips for dieters are Onion-Dill Dip and Zucchini Dip, both of which call for low-fat yogurt.

Many of the dip recipes on the following pages include suggestions for compatible accompaniments from the vegetable family. Presentation and serving suggestions for raw vegetables appear in the Bagna Cauda picture on page 16; the recipe plan is on page 14. And with a little experimenting, you'll accumulate a collection of your own favorite combinations.

Party spreads are a clever party-giver's best friend. Made ahead and chilled, they can be waiting on a coffee table for the first guest's arrival, and without further attention, can last throughout the party. In addition to pâtés, cheese balls, and fish-based spreads, you'll find information on how to make your own Fresh Creamy Cheese, which can be eaten as is, spiced with savory herbs, or studded with toasted nuts as pictured on page 21.

Creamy melted cheese, piping hot and golden, is the basis for most of the fondue recipes. In addition to the classic Swiss Fondue, you'll find Italian, Swiss, and Mexican variations on this hearty appetizer theme.

Guacamole with pomegranate seeds (page 11).

Romaine spears and raw mushrooms become out-of-hand salad when dipped into Green Goddess—one course from "Nothing-to-It Party." For party plan, see pages 70–71. Recipe for Green Goddess Dip on page 12.

dips

THAI CHILE SAUCE

Raw apple, chiles, and anchovy paste are just three of the unlikely ingredients that combine to make this authentic Thai dip, called *nam prik*, for raw vegetables.

Choose an assortment of vegetables—such as carrot sticks, cucumber rounds, green pepper strips, and whole green onions—and arrange on a tray around the chile sauce.

> ½ cup finely shredded green apple (squeeze out excess liquid)
> 1 to 2 tablespoons seeded and finely chopped canned California green chiles
> 2 teaspoons *each* brown sugar and anchovy paste
> 1 teaspoon grated lime peel
> 2 tablespoons lime juice
> ½ teaspoon salt
> 2 tablespoons finely chopped green onion (tops included)

Combine apple, chiles, brown sugar, anchovy paste, lime peel, lime juice, and salt. Stir until blended. Pour into a small dish and sprinkle with onion. Makes about ½ cup.

ZIPPY CLAM DIP

Crisp raw vegetables make perfect partners for this spicy dip.

> 1 can (6½ oz.) minced clams
> 1 large package (8 oz.) cream cheese, softened
> 2 tablespoons finely minced parsley
> 1 tablespoon minced onion
> 2 teaspoons *each* lemon juice and prepared horseradish
> 1 teaspoon seasoning salt
> Pepper

Drain clams, reserving liquid. Add 3 tablespoons clam liquid (if necessary, add milk to make this amount) to cream cheese; beat until creamy smooth. Stir in clams, parsley, onion, lemon juice, horseradish, seasoning salt, and pepper to taste; mix

thoroughly. Cover and chill at least 2 hours.

To serve, surround with a variety of raw vegetables cut into chunks for dipping. Makes about 2 cups.

ANCHOIADE PROVENÇAL

In the south of France, a pungent anchovy-garlic sauce known as *anchoiade* is served as a dip for raw and cooked vegetables and hard-cooked eggs or as a first-course spread on bread.

Good vegetable accompaniments are celery or cucumber sticks, green onions, radishes, cherry tomatoes, whole mushrooms, or artichoke hearts that have been cooked, drained, and chilled.

> 3 cans (2 oz. *each*) flat anchovy fillets, well drained
> ¼ cup red wine vinegar
> ¾ cup olive oil
> 4 cloves garlic, minced or pressed
> ¼ teaspoon pepper
> ½ cup chopped parsley

Put anchovies and vinegar in a blender and whirl until puréed. Add oil, garlic, and pepper; whirl until smoothly blended; stir in parsley. Transfer to a serving

bowl; cover and chill at least 2 hours. Makes 2 cups.

DIPS FROM THE SEA

A shellfish dip surrounded by a variety of crisp raw vegetables makes a festive and delicious beginning for a spring dinner party. Take your choice of shrimp or crab for the dip and offer three or four vegetables, such as cauliflowerets, sliced zucchini, carrot or celery sticks, red or green pepper strips, or cherry tomatoes.

Shrimp Dip

> 1 large package (8 oz.) cream cheese, softened
> ¼ cup sour cream
> 1 tablespoon lemon juice
> 3 tablespoons thinly sliced green onion
> ¼ to ½ teaspoon crushed red pepper
> 1 tablespoon milk
> ½ pound small, cooked shrimp
> Salt
> 1 to 2 tablespoons toasted slivered almonds

Beat together cream cheese and sour cream until smooth and fluffy. Stir in lemon juice, green onion, red pepper, milk, and shrimp (reserve a few for garnish). Season to taste with salt.

Cover and chill 2 to 4 hours to blend flavors.

Just before serving, stir gently, turn into a serving dish, and top with reserved shrimp and almonds. Surround with a variety of crisp raw vegetables. Makes about 2 cups.

Pacific Crab Dip. Prepare Shrimp Dip according to preceding directions but omit red pepper and shrimp; substitute 1 small clove garlic (minced or pressed) and ½ pound crab meat (flaked). Makes about 2 cups.

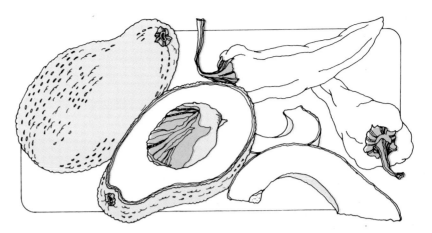

AVOCADO DIP WITH RED AND BLACK CAVIAR

A dollop of caviar transforms a simple avocado into an elegant dip in its own natural container.

   1 large ripe avocado
   ¼ cup sour cream
   2 tablespoons lime juice
   ⅛ teaspoon salt
   2 tablespoons *each* black and red caviar

Split avocado in half lengthwise, remove pit, and carefully scoop out pulp, preserving shell. Thoroughly mash pulp. Stir in sour cream, lime juice, and salt until blended. Spoon into half shells.

With back of spoon, make a cavity in center of each mound of avocado; fill hollow of one with black caviar, the other with red caviar. Serve with crackers or tortilla chips. Makes about 1½ cups.

REFRIED BEAN DIP

A quiet corner of a hot barbecue can be used to keep this dip warm. Or set it in a chafing dish over hot water.

   1 can (1 lb.) refried beans
   1 cup (4 oz.) shredded Cheddar cheese
   ½ cup chopped green onion
   ¼ teaspoon salt
   2 to 3 tablespoons taco sauce

In a small pan or heatproof pottery bowl, stir together beans, cheese, onion, salt, and taco sauce until well blended. Place over medium heat, stirring constantly, just until heated throughout. Serve warm with crisp-fried tortillas (page 15) or tortilla chips. Makes about 3 cups.

GUACAMOLE

(Pictured on page 9)

A favorite of many westerners, guacamole has as many variations as it has admirers. Everyone has a preferred seasoning or two, but the basic avocado and citrus mixture usually remains the same. The citrus is a must, for it keeps the avocado from discoloring.

   2 large ripe avocados
   2 to 3 tablespoons lemon or lime juice (or to taste)
     About ½ teaspoon salt
   2 to 4 canned California green chiles, seeded and chopped *or* several drops liquid hot pepper seasoning

Cut avocados in half, remove pit, and scoop out pulp. Coarsely mash pulp with a fork. Stir in lemon juice, salt, chiles, and hot pepper seasoning. (Or, for a smooth dip, whirl in a blender.) Serve with crisp-fried tortillas (page 15) or tortilla chips. Makes about 1⅔ cups.

Variations. For a change of pace, try seasoning guacamole in any of the following ways:

Add 1 clove garlic (minced or pressed) or 2 to 3 tablespoons minced onion—or add both garlic and onion.

Stir in ½ teaspoon ground coriander or 2 teaspoons minced fresh coriander (cilantro).

Mix in 1 pimento, chopped, or as much as 1 tomato, chopped.

For a festive appearance, garnish with tomato wedges and fresh coriander (cilantro) or parsley sprigs, or sprinkle pomegranate seeds over the top.

PEANUT SAUCE

An unusual combination of textures and flavors makes up this Malaysian dip, called *rojak*. In oriental markets you'll find jícama and tofu puffs—two accompaniments for this sauce.

   ⅓ cup crunchy peanut butter
   3 tablespoons firmly packed brown sugar
   ½ teaspoon crushed red pepper
   ¼ cup lemon juice
   2 tablespoons tomato-based chile sauce or catsup
   ½ teaspoon soy sauce

Mix peanut butter, brown sugar, red pepper, lemon juice, chile sauce, and soy sauce until well blended. Store at room temperature until next day, if desired. Serve with raw vegetables—cucumber or jícama slices, celery stalks, carrot or green pepper strips—or with pineapple chunks or fried tofu puffs. Makes about ¾ cup.

ROQUEFORT AND SOUR CREAM DIP

Roquefort salad dressing, a perennial favorite, was the inspiration for this ever-popular dip. To allow the flavors to blend and mellow, prepare it a few hours in advance.

   1 cup sour cream
   ⅓ cup mayonnaise
   3 tablespoons lemon juice
   1 package (4 oz.) Roquefort, crumbled
   1 clove garlic, minced or pressed
   ½ teaspoon salt

Place sour cream, mayonnaise, lemon juice, cheese, garlic, and salt in a blender; whirl until smoothly puréed. Refrigerate several hours or until next day. Serve with crisp crackers or raw vegetables. Makes about 2 cups.

BLENDER HOLLANDAISE

A rushed hostess will appreciate this easy-to-make hollandaise sauce, which can be prepared at the last minute. Serve it with cooked, chilled artichokes or fresh, raw vegetables.

   3 egg yolks, at room temperature
  1½ tablespoons lemon juice
   ¾ cup butter or margarine
   1 tablespoon hot water
   ½ teaspoon salt
    Dash of cayenne
   1 teaspoon prepared mustard

Put egg yolks and lemon juice in a blender. Melt butter and heat until it bubbles—don't brown. Add hot water to egg yolks and lemon juice; turn blender on high speed and immediately pour in hot butter in a steady stream (takes about 5 seconds).

Add salt, cayenne, and mustard; whirl until well blended (about 30 seconds). Makes about 2 cups.

Hollandaise with Cucumber or Shrimp. Prepare hollandaise as directed above. Stir in 1 table-

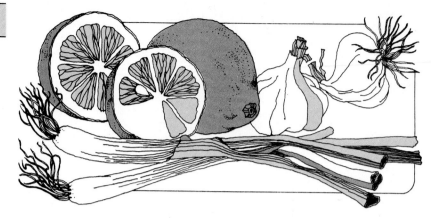

spoon *each* chopped parsley and chives. Then add either 1 cucumber (peeled, seeded, and chopped) or 1 can (about 5 oz.) shrimp, rinsed and drained.

GREEN GODDESS DIP

(Pictured on page 9)

The classic salad dressing, Green Goddess, can double as a delicious change-of-pace dip for raw vegetables. It is especially good with mushrooms and romaine spears.

   1 clove garlic
   ¼ cup *each* coarsely chopped parsley, green onion, and watercress
   ½ teaspoon onion salt
   1 teaspoon *each* tarragon leaves and anchovy paste
   2 teaspoons lemon juice
   ½ cup *each* mayonnaise and sour cream

In a blender, put garlic, parsley, green onion, watercress, onion salt, tarragon, anchovy paste, and lemon juice; whirl until smoothly puréed. Stir in mayonnaise and sour cream until smooth. Makes 1½ cups.

ONION-DILL DIP

You can make this dip into a low-calorie specialty by preparing it with low-fat yogurt instead of sour cream.

Serve the dip with vegetables —cherry tomatoes, carrots, celery,

radishes, cauliflower—or with cooked, chilled shrimp.

  2½ cups sour cream or low-fat or regular plain yogurt
   1 package (amount for 4 servings) dry onion soup mix
   1 tablespoon minced parsley
   ¼ teaspoon garlic powder
   1 teaspoon dill weed
    Dash of pepper

Stir together sour cream, onion soup mix, parsley, garlic powder, dill weed, and pepper until well blended. Chill at least 1 hour. Makes about 3 cups.

BACON AND COTTAGE CHEESE DIP

You can please calorie counters if you serve this dip with vegetables instead of chips.

  16 slices bacon
   2 cups cottage cheese
   ¼ teaspoon garlic powder
    Dash of cayenne
   1 teaspoon onion salt
   2 teaspoons lemon juice
   ¼ cup mayonnaise or sour cream
   5 teaspoons milk

Cook bacon in a frying pan over medium heat until crisp; when cool, crumble and reserve. In blender, put cottage cheese, garlic powder, cayenne, onion salt, lemon juice, mayonnaise, and milk; whirl until smoothly blended; then stir in crumbled bacon. Cover and chill. Makes about 2½ cups.

CURRY DIP

(Pictured on page 4)

The amount of curry you use to spice this dip will determine if it's meek and mild or aggressively adventurous.

½ cup sour cream
3 tablespoons mayonnaise
½ teaspoon curry powder (or to taste)
⅛ teaspoon cayenne
1 tablespoon catsup
¼ teaspoon Worcestershire
Dash of salt
1 clove garlic, minced or pressed

Stir together sour cream, mayonnaise, curry powder, cayenne, catsup, Worcestershire, salt, and garlic until blended. Refrigerate at least 4 hours or until next day to allow flavors to blend. Stir before serving. Makes about 1 cup.

MOROCCAN EGGPLANT DIP

Spicy hot and flavored with fresh coriander, this dip is a simmered mixture of eggplant, tomato sauce, and green pepper. Serve it chilled to scoop on bread, such as Arab pocket bread (cut in wedges), slices of French bread, or dark, firm pumpernickel; or, accompany the dip with raw vegetables, such as zucchini or cucumber slices, carrot or green pepper sticks.

1 large (about 1½ lb.) eggplant
3 tablespoons olive oil
1 can (8 oz.) tomato sauce
2 cloves garlic, minced or pressed
1 green pepper, seeded and chopped
1 tablespoon ground cumin
¼ teaspoon cayenne
2 teaspoons *each* sugar and salt
¼ cup red wine vinegar
¼ cup chopped fresh coriander (cilantro) *or* 2 tablespoons dried cilantro leaves

Dice eggplant, discarding ends. In a large frying pan, heat oil over medium-high heat; add eggplant, tomato sauce, garlic, green pep-

per, cumin, cayenne, sugar, salt, and vinegar. Cook, covered, over medium heat for 20 minutes. Uncover and boil mixture over high heat, stirring, until reduced to about 3 cups. Cover and chill at least 2 hours or until next day. Before serving, stir in coriander. Makes 3 cups.

VEGETABLE-BASED DIPS

Dipping vegetables in a vegetable-based sauce—it's hard to imagine a lighter or more refreshing appetizer. You can serve these two dips separately or together, for both complement the same fresh raw vegetables, such as cauliflower, cherry tomatoes, mushrooms, green or red peppers, radishes, or zucchini.

To serve, gather rinsed whole vegetables in a basket, accompany with a knife, and invite guests to cut off portions.

Both dips can be made a few hours ahead but keep them covered and cold.

Zucchini Dip

Finely shred enough zucchini to make 1 cup, firmly packed. Place zucchini in a wire strainer and press out excess moisture. Mix zucchini with ¼ cup unflavored yogurt, 2 cloves garlic (minced or pressed), and salt to taste. Cover and chill at least 1 hour to blend flavors. Stir before serving. Makes about 1 cup.

Cucumber Chile Dip

Peel and mince 1 large cucumber; mix in ½ teaspoon salt and chill at least 1 hour to release liquid. Smoothly blend 1 small package (3 oz.) cream cheese with 2 tablespoons sour cream. Drain all liquid from cucumber; combine cucumber with cream cheese mixture. Stir in 2 tablespoons seeded and chopped canned California green chiles and salt to taste. Cover and chill. Makes 1 cup.

CHILE CON QUESO

Keep this dip warm in a chafing dish over hot water and serve with tortillas.

2 medium-size onions, chopped
2 tablespoons salad oil
2 cans (7 oz. *each*) diced California green chiles
1 teaspoon salt
1 small can (about 5 oz.) evaporated milk
2 cups (8 oz.) shredded jack or Longhorn Cheddar cheese

Cook onions in salad oil over medium-low heat until very soft. Add chiles and salt and simmer, stirring, until juices have evaporated (about 5 minutes). Add milk and simmer gently, stirring, until slightly thickened (about 4 minutes). Remove from heat, cool about 2 minutes, add shredded cheese, and cover until cheese melts. Then stir and serve hot. Makes about 4 cups.

BAGNA CAUDA—
SERVE-YOURSELF ITALIAN-STYLE APPETIZER
(Pictured on page 16)

This colorful appetizer is so straightforward it almost belies its goodness. It's just plain raw vegetables dipped, but not cooked, in a mutually shared bowl of bubbling butter and olive oil, made bold by garlic and anchovies.

The artistry, freshness, and ease of Bagna Cauda make it ideal for casual entertaining. And the adaptability of the ingredients lets you scale an appetizer course to fit a group of 8 to 30.

How to Serve Bagna Cauda
Prepare the vegetables according to the following directions. Because you want to keep that right-from-the-garden look, do just enough cutting so that it will be easy for guests to break away portions to eat.

Arrange vegetables in a basket of appropriate size. Place alongside it the hot butter-oil sauce (recipe follows). And present a basket of thinly sliced French bread or sliced crusty rolls.

To eat, swirl a piece of vegetable through the hot sauce. Hold a piece of bread like a napkin under the vegetable to catch drips as you lift it. Eventually, the bread soaks up enough drippings to become a tasty bit itself.

Keep in mind that people are often able to consume an astonishing quantity of Bagna Cauda—it's easy to justify taking your fill of the fresh, crisp vegetables because very little of the rich sauce actually sticks to each morsel.

Bagna Cauda Vegetables
You'll need about 1 to 2 cups vegetable pieces per person, but you'll have to estimate quantities while vegetables are still whole. Choose a colorful assortment. If you wash and prepare vegetables early in the day, store them in plastic bags or wrap with clear plastic film and refrigerate as long as 6 to 8 hours. Sprinkle with water just before serving.

Artichokes. Cook artichokes as directed on page 61. To eat, bite off tender base of each bract.

Cabbage. Cut red or white cabbage in half. Cut vertical gashes in each half. Break off chunks to eat.

Carrots. Leave on an inch of stem; peel. Gash carrot not quite through in short sections; break apart to eat.

Cauliflower. Cut out core, keeping head whole. Break off flowerets to eat.

Cherry tomatoes. Dip with stems.

Green peppers. Cut pepper vertically down to stem in 8 to 12 sections around seed center. Break to eat.

Mushrooms. Trim stem ends. Eat small mushrooms whole. Cut large ones through cap only into 4 or 6 sections; break to eat.

Radishes. Cut off root ends and all but 1 or 2 leaves to hold for dipping.

Zucchini and yellow crookneck squash. Trim ends; cut not quite through in short sections. Break apart to eat.

Hot Butter-Oil Sauce
Choose a heatproof container that will be only about half filled by quantity of sauce you make. In it, combine ½ cup (¼ lb.) butter, ¼ cup olive oil, and 4 small cloves garlic (minced or pressed). Drain 1 can (2 oz.) flat anchovy fillets on paper towels and finely chop; add to sauce and stir over moderate heat until mixture bubbles.

To serve, set over candle or low alcohol flame. Mixture must not get hot enough to brown and burn. Makes 8 to 10 servings (double recipe for 16 to 20 servings, triple recipe for 24 to 30 servings).

NACHOS

(Pictured on Front Cover)

The colorful and distinctive dish shown on our cover, nachos, can be made simply with fried tortilla pieces, cheese, and chiles for zip, or with any combination of the ingredients listed in the Super Nachos recipe. When made with all the choices for the base and garnishes, the result can be appetizers for a dozen or more, or a meal for 4 to 6 people.

Both are dishes you eat out of hand, using tortillas to scoop up the savory center.

Basic Nachos

    6 to 8 cups crisp-fried tortilla
        pieces (directions follow) or
        corn-flavored chips
      About 4 cups (1 lb.) shredded
        jack or mild Cheddar cheese (or
        half of each)
    1 can (4 oz.) whole California
        green chiles (for mildest flavor,
        remove seeds and pith),
        chopped

Spread tortilla pieces about one layer deep (they overlap) in each of 2 low-rimmed 10 or 11-inch round pans or ovenproof plates. Sprinkle tortillas evenly with cheese; then top with chiles.

Place both pans, uncovered, in a 400° oven for about 5 minutes or until cheese melts (or bake in sequence so you can replenish the first serving with another hot one). Serve at once, picking up tortilla pieces with your fingers; if desired, keep nachos hot on an electric warming tray. Makes 6 to 8 appetizer servings.

Crisp-fried Tortilla Pieces. Arrange 12 corn tortillas (1 package) in a stack and cut into 6 equal wedges. Pour about ½ inch salad oil in a deep 2 or 3-quart pan and set on medium-high to high heat. When oil is hot enough to make a piece of tortilla sizzle (350° to 375°), add tortilla pieces, a stack at a time, stirring to separate. Cook until crisp (1 to 1½ minutes); lift from oil with slotted spoon and drain on paper towels. Repeat procedure until all tortilla pieces

are cooked. If you like, sprinkle lightly with salt. Store pieces airtight if made ahead. Makes about 8 cups.

Super Nachos

    ½ pound *each* lean ground beef and
        chorizo sausage, casing re-
        moved (or use only lean ground
        beef—1 pound total)
    1 large onion, chopped
      Salt
      Liquid hot pepper seasoning
    1 or 2 cans (about 1 lb. *each*) re-
        fried beans
    1 can (4 oz.) whole California
        green chiles (for mildest flavor,
        remove seeds and pith),
        chopped
    2 to 3 cups shredded jack or mild
        Cheddar cheese
    ¾ cup prepared taco sauce (green or
        red)
      Garnishes (suggestions follow)
    8 cups crisp-fried tortilla pieces or
        corn-flavored chips

Crumble ground beef and sausage in a frying pan. Add onion and cook on high heat, stirring, until meat is lightly browned. Discard fat; season with salt and liquid hot pepper seasoning to taste.

Spread beans in a shallow 10 by 15-inch oval or rectangular pan or ovenproof dish (or one of equivalent area). Top evenly with meat. Sprinkle chiles over bean and meat mixture, cover evenly with cheese, and drizzle with taco sauce. Cover and chill if made ahead. Bake, uncovered, in a 400° oven for 20 to 25 minutes or until very hot throughout.

Remove from oven and quickly garnish with some or all of the following: about ¼ cup chopped green onion (including some tops)

and about 1 cup pitted ripe olives; in the center mound 1 can (about 8 oz.) thawed avocado dip (or 1 medium-size ripe avocado, peeled, pitted, and coarsely mashed) and top with about 1 cup sour cream; add a mild, red pickled pepper and fresh coriander (cilantro) or parsley sprigs.

Then quickly tuck about 8 cups fried tortilla pieces (see preceding directions) or corn-flavored chips just around edges of bean mixture (making a petaled flower effect) and serve at once.

Scoop up bean mixture with tortilla pieces; if desired, keep platter hot on an electric warming tray while serving. Makes 10 to 12 appetizer servings.

GREEN CHILE CHEESE DIP

For the tender-mouthed, the green chiles in this recipe can be cut back by as much as half.

    1 can (4 oz.) diced California green
        chiles
    1 cup sour cream
    ½ cup finely chopped onion
    1 large package (8 oz.) cream
        cheese, softened
      Half-and-half (light cream) or
        milk

Add chiles, sour cream, and onion to cream cheese and beat with a mixer until well blended. Add enough half-and-half to get correct dipping consistency. Cover and refrigerate for several hours to blend. Serve with crisp-fried tortillas (see preceding recipe, Nachos) or corn-flavored chips. Makes about 3 cups.

Hot, buttery garlic
and anchovy sauce makes a
bold dip for fresh raw vegetables.
(Recipe on page 14)

spreads

ARMENIAN HOMMUS

(Pictured on page 76)

To make this unusual spread, you can start with a product called *hommus*—or with a can of garbanzo beans.

Hommus, sold in Armenian markets, can be used directly from the can, but its flavor is enhanced when a few fresh ingredients are added (see following directions).

With a blender, though, you can easily make the spread from canned garbanzos and either sesame paste (called *tahine*) or sesame seed and oil.

Armenians present hommus in this way: they smooth the top and then use a small spatula to mark a design; when olive oil (about 1 tablespoon) is drizzled over, it pools in the depressions. If you prefer, you can garnish this spread with chopped parsley or garbanzos.

To serve hommus, spread on slices of doughnut-shaped Greek bread (called *kouloura*) or any sweet French bread.

- 1 **can (15 oz.) garbanzos, drained (reserve liquid)**
- 2 **tablespoons** *each* **toasted sesame seed and sesame oil (or use olive oil and increase sesame seed to ¼ cup)**
- 3 **tablespoons lemon juice**
- 1 **large clove garlic**
- ¼ **teaspoon ground cumin (optional)**
  Salt and pepper

Put garbanzos into a blender. Add sesame seed and sesame oil, lemon juice, garlic, and cumin. Pour in ¼ cup garbanzo liquid and whirl, starting and stopping motor and adding more liquid, if needed, until mixture is smooth and the consistency of heavy batter. Season to taste with salt and pepper. Garnish as suggested above. Makes about 1½ cups.

To Make Hommus with Tahine.
Omit sesame seed and oil; use ¼ cup sesame paste (tahine).

To Serve Prepared Hommus.
Turn 1 can (15 oz.) hommus into a bowl and stir in 1 tablespoon lemon juice, 1 clove garlic (minced or pressed), ¼ teaspoon ground cumin (optional), salt and pepper to taste. Garnish as suggested.

EGGPLANT SPREAD

You bake an eggplant until it collapses, then blend it with olive oil and green onion for a tasty spread to serve with crisp Melba toast or slices of party-style rye bread.

- 1 **large (about 1½ lb.) eggplant**
- 2 **tablespoons** *each* **minced green onion and catsup**
- ¼ **cup olive oil**
- 1 **tablespoon red wine vinegar**
- ¾ **teaspoon salt**
- ¼ **teaspoon pepper**
  Minced parsley

With a fork, pierce skin of eggplant; place in rimmed pan. Bake in a 400° oven for 1 hour or until soft. Cool; split skin and scoop out interior into a bowl. Add onion, catsup, olive oil, vinegar, salt, and pepper; stir until creamy.

Cover and chill if made ahead. Garnish with minced parsley and serve at room temperature. Makes about 2½ cups.

DILL TUNA MOLD

Use a 2-cup fish-shaped mold if you have one. It makes a pretty presentation for a tasty spread that uses just one can of tuna.

- 1 **envelope unflavored gelatin**
- 2 **tablespoons lemon juice**
- 1 **chicken bouillon cube dissolved in ½ cup boiling water**
- ½ **cup mayonnaise**
- ¼ **cup milk**
- 2 **tablespoons chopped parsley**
- 1 **tablespoon minced green onion**
- 1 **teaspoon** *each* **dry mustard and dill weed**
- ¼ **teaspoon pepper**
- 1 **can (9¼ oz.) tuna, well drained**
- ½ **cup shredded cucumber**

In a bowl stir together gelatin and lemon juice; let stand 5 minutes to soften. Stir in chicken broth to dissolve completely. In a large bowl, mix together mayonnaise, milk, parsley, green onion, mustard, dill weed, pepper, tuna, and cucumber; stir in gelatin mixture. Pour into a 2-cup mold and chill until set (about 2 hours). Unmold onto a serving platter. Garnish with parsley and serve with Melba toast or salted wheat crackers. Makes 2 cups.

CRAB AND WATER CHESTNUT SPREAD

Serve this refreshing and crunchy appetizer spread on crisp shredded wheat crackers.

- 1 **pound crab meat, chopped or shredded**
- ½ **cup minced water chestnuts**
- 2 **tablespoons soy sauce**
- ½ **cup mayonnaise**
- 2 **tablespoons minced green onion**

Combine crab meat with water chestnuts, soy, mayonnaise, and onion. Cover and chill as long as 8 hours. Makes about 3 cups.

SMOKED OYSTER AND CHEESE SPREAD

Crisp toast rounds are a good base for this smoked oyster cheese. Let guests spread their own so appetizers will be crisp.

- 1 **small package (3 oz.) cream cheese, softened**
- 1 **small jar (4 oz.) smoked oysters, drained and chopped**
- 1 **tablespoon mayonnaise**
- 1 **tablespoon dry Sherry or milk**
- 1 **teaspoon onion juice**
- ½ **teaspoon paprika**
  Chives, finely minced

Mix cheese, oysters, mayonnaise, Sherry, onion juice, and paprika. Pile into a serving dish. Chill. Sprinkle with chives and serve. Makes 1 cup.

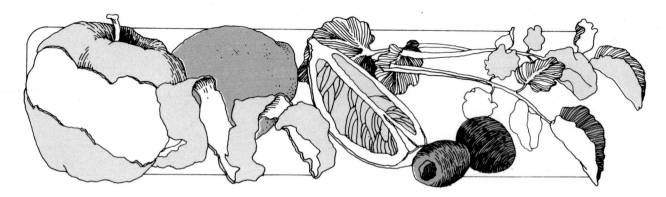

SMOKED SALMON SPREAD

Delightfully simple, this fish spread will appeal to busy hostesses. You begin with canned salmon and cream cheese, two good items to keep on hand for last-minute entertaining.

1 can (about 4 oz.) smoked salmon, drained
1 small package (3 oz.) cream cheese, softened
1 small clove garlic, minced or pressed
Salt and pepper
Green onion

In a small bowl, break salmon with a fork until finely flaked. Add cream cheese and garlic, mix well, and season with salt and pepper. Spoon into bowl or mound on plate; cover and chill 30 minutes or until next day. To serve, garnish with sliced green onion and accompany with Melba toast or other crisp unsalted crackers. Makes about 1 cup.

SPICY CLAM SPREAD

You can serve this low-calorie spread on Melba toast for tempting hot appetizers.

⅓ cup small curd cottage cheese
¼ teaspoon Worcestershire
1 tablespoon mayonnaise
1½ teaspoons lemon or lime juice
⅛ teaspoon *each* garlic salt and liquid hot pepper seasoning
1 can (8 oz.) minced clams, drained
Salt and pepper
14 to 16 pieces Melba toast
Chopped parsley

In a blender, combine cottage cheese, Worcestershire, mayonnaise, lemon juice, garlic salt, and hot pepper seasoning; whirl until well blended and smooth. Stir in clams and salt and pepper to taste. Cover and refrigerate if made ahead.

Just before serving, spread mixture on Melba toast. Place on a cooky sheet in a preheated broiler about 3 inches from heat. Broil until mixture is bubbly and heated through (about 3 minutes). Sprinkle parsley evenly over tops and serve at once. Makes 14 to 16 appetizers.

MOLDED CHICKEN LIVER PÂTÉ

Shimmering gelatin makes an attractive topping for this molded chicken liver pâté. To unmold, dip it in hot water for about 5 seconds, then tap the edge of the mold sharply to free the pâté. Repeat if necessary.

¼ teaspoon unflavored gelatin
¼ cup *each* water and condensed consommé
¾ pound chicken livers
Water
¾ cup butter or margarine, softened
3 tablespoons finely chopped onion
1 teaspoon dry mustard
¼ teaspoon *each* salt, ground nutmeg, and anchovy paste
Dash *each* cayenne and ground cloves
Lemon slices and watercress for garnish

In a small pan, soften gelatin in the ¼ cup water. Add consommé and heat, stirring occasionally, until gelatin is completely dissolved. Pour into a 2½ to 3-cup mold; chill until firm.

Cover livers with water; bring to a boil and simmer for about 20 minutes or until livers are very tender when pierced with a fork. Cool slightly in liquid.

Drain livers and whirl in blender with butter until mixture is very smooth and fluffy (or press livers through a food mill or strainer; add butter and beat until smooth). Blend in onion, mustard, salt, nutmeg, anchovy paste, cayenne, and cloves. Spread over gelatin in mold, pressing liver mixture in evenly; cover and chill until firm. Unmold onto serving plate; garnish with lemon slices and watercress. Serve with crisp crackers. Makes about 2½ cups.

CREAMY PÂTÉ

You can use either chicken or turkey livers to make this pâté, distinguished by the addition of apples, ripe olives, and hard-cooked eggs. Serve on crisp crackers.

½ cup butter or margarine
1 cup *each* diced onion and diced, peeled apple
1 pound chicken or turkey livers, cut in half
½ cup dry Sherry or Sauterne
4 hard-cooked eggs, chopped
1 can (4½ oz.) chopped ripe olives
½ teaspoon salt
¼ teaspoon pepper
2 dashes liquid hot pepper seasoning

In a frying pan, melt butter over medium heat, then add onion, apple, and livers. Cook, stirring, until onion is limp. Add Sherry and cook, uncovered, over medium heat until liquid is reduced by half (about 5 minutes). Cool briefly.

Whirl a small amount of liver mixture in a blender until smooth; add more of mixture and whirl again. Continue adding mixture and whirling until all liver mixture is puréed. Then add eggs and olives and whirl until smoothly blended. (Or use the fine blade of a food chopper and grind liver mixture with eggs and olives.)

Stir in salt, pepper, and hot pepper seasoning. Cover and chill at least 3 hours or as long as 1 week. Makes about 4 cups.

LIVERWURST PÂTÉ

The basis of this pâté is liver-flavored sausage. It is especially good spread on Melba toast.

1 package (8 oz.) liver-flavored sausage
6 slices crisp cooked bacon, crumbled
2 tablespoons finely chopped green onion, including some tops
1 tablespoon dry Sherry
2 tablespoons butter or margarine, softened

Mash liver sausage with a fork. Stir in bacon, onion, Sherry, and butter until well blended. Cover and chill as long as 1 week. Before serving, let soften at room temperature at least 1 hour. Makes about 1 cup.

RUMAKI SPREAD

The flavors of the popular Japanese hot appetizer, *rumaki*, are retained in this chicken liver spread. Crisp bacon and water chestnuts, added at the last, make it crunchy. Let the spread come to room temperature, then serve with crisp crackers.

½ cup (¼ lb.) butter or margarine
½ pound chicken livers
1 tablespoon soy sauce
½ teaspoon *each* onion salt and dry mustard
¼ teaspoon nutmeg
Dash cayenne
1 can (5 oz.) water chestnuts, well drained and finely chopped
6 slices crisp cooked bacon, crumbled
Green onions, thinly sliced

In a frying pan over medium heat, melt butter. Add chicken livers and cook, stirring, until livers are firm but still slightly pink inside (cut to test). Put liver mixture, soy, onion salt, mustard, nutmeg, and cayenne in a blender; whirl until smoothly puréed, stirring as needed. Stir in water chestnuts and bacon. Refrigerate at least 2 hours or until next day to blend flavors. For easy spreading, let soften at room temperature for at least an hour. Garnish with onions. Makes about 1½ cups.

FRESH CREAMY CHEESE
(Pictured on page 21)

Making your own fresh cheese is lots of fun and surprisingly easy—it takes just a few minutes of care for about 4 days. A soft cream cheese, it's perfect to use as is with fresh fruit (such as seedless grapes) and crackers or as a substitute in any recipes calling for cream cheese—such as the spreads on pages 15–23.

Start with either skim or whole milk or light or heavy cream. Skim milk makes a tart but surprisingly rich-tasting cheese; cream makes velvety, cool-tasting cheese; whole milk and light cream produce subtle variations within this range.

2 quarts skim or whole milk *or* 1 quart half-and-half (light cream) *or* 3 cups whipping cream
2 tablespoons buttermilk if you use half-and-half or whipping cream *or* ¼ cup buttermilk if you use skim or whole milk

In a pan over low heat, heat milk to lukewarm (90° to 100°), then pour into bowl. Stir in buttermilk. Cover and keep at room temperature 24 to 48 hours or until a soft curd is formed (mixture looks like a soft yogurt). Curd forms faster on hot days than on cool ones.

Line a colander with a clean muslin cloth; set in sink. Pour in curd and let drain about 10 minutes. Fold cloth over curd. Set colander on a rack in a rimmed baking pan (for milk curd, allow 1 inch between rack and pan bottom). Make whole unit airtight with clear plastic film. Let curd drain in refrigerator for 36 to 48 hours.

Spoon drained curd from cloth into a bowl and stir in ¾ teaspoon salt until blended; discard whey accumulated beneath colander.

Makes 2 cups cheese.

BOTTOMLESS CHEESE CROCK

Once this cheese crock is started, you keep it going by blending cheese remnants into it. And if additions keep pace with subtractions, you'll have a cheese spread that lasts almost indefinitely.

Store the crock in the refrigerator. Before serving, let cheese soften at room temperature for about an hour.

    4 cups (1 lb.) shredded sharp
        Cheddar cheese
    1 small package (3 oz.) cream
        cheese
1½ tablespoons olive oil
    1 teaspoon *each* dry mustard and
        garlic salt
    2 tablespoons brandy

Let cheeses stand at room temperature until soft. Then combine them and add olive oil, mustard, garlic salt, and brandy; beat until well blended. Pack into container, cover, and refrigerate for about a week before using the first time. Makes about 3 cups.

Adding to the Crock. Firm cheeses—such as Swiss, jack, or any Cheddar types—are fine. Shred and beat in while cheese in crock is soft, adding small amounts of olive oil or cream cheese for good consistency. Also add brandy, dry Sherry, Port, beer, or Kirsch, keeping the total not larger than the original proportion of brandy. Then let mixture age a few days before serving. Use it every week or two, saving part of original mixture to keep crock going.

COOL AND REFRESHING APPETIZER MOLDS

These sour cream and avocado cream molds are especially convenient for a busy hostess because they can be assembled a day ahead. Refrigerate them until almost ready to use, then unmold and garnish an hour or so before the guests are due. The creams retain their forms neatly for several hours at room temperature.

Sour Cream Mold

    1 envelope unflavored gelatin
    ¼ cup cold water
    1 tablespoon white wine vinegar
    2 cups sour cream
    2 jars (4 oz. *each*) red or black cav-
        iar (or use one of each)
    3 or 4 green onions, thinly sliced
        (including some tops)

In a pan sprinkle gelatin over water and let stand 5 minutes to soften. Heat, stirring, until gelatin is dissolved. Add vinegar and sour cream and stir until thoroughly blended and smooth. Pour into a mold at least 3-cup size; cover and chill until set.

To serve, unmold. Drain caviars separately in a fine wire strainer. Garnish top of mold with caviar and onions, keeping each of the elements separate. Guests spoon small portions on Melba toast or on unsalted wheat or rye crackers. Makes about 3 cups.

Molded Avocado Cream

    1 envelope unflavored gelatin
    ¼ cup cold water
    ¼ teaspoon salt
    2 tablespoons finely chopped
        parsley or chives
        Dash liquid hot pepper season-
        ing
    1 cup sour cream
    1 can (about 8 oz.) frozen avocado
        dip, thawed
        Parsley sprigs
        About ½ pound small cooked
        shrimp
        Melba toast or unsalted wheat or
        rye crackers

In a pan sprinkle gelatin over water and let stand 5 minutes to soften. Heat, stirring, until gelatin is dissolved. Add salt, parsley, hot pepper seasoning, sour cream, and avocado dip and stir until thoroughly blended and smooth. Pour into a mold at least 3-cup size; cover and chill until set.

To serve, unmold. Garnish with parsley sprigs and surround with shrimp and Melba toast. Guests spoon some of the avocado cream onto a piece of Melba toast and top with a few shrimp. Makes about 2 cups.

CAMEMBERT SPREAD

You might pile this spread into a lettuce shell and garnish it with thinly sliced radishes. It is especially good with Melba rye toast or cocktail rye bread.

    1 large package (8 oz.) cream
        cheese, softened
    1 package (4 oz.) soft Camembert
        cheese
    2 cups small curd cottage cheese
    ⅓ cup grated Parmesan cheese
        About 1 teaspoon seasoned salt
        Toasted sesame seed or dill seed
        (optional)

Beat together cream cheese and Camembert (including skin) until smooth. Combine with cottage cheese, Parmesan cheese, and seasoned salt to taste. Sprinkle sesame or dill seed on top, if you wish. Makes about 3½ cups.

CREAM CHEESE TRIO

Here is a simple way to use cream cheese for a triple effect. Arrange the cheese spreads on a narrow tray and replenish taco and soy sauces as needed.

    3 small packages (3 oz. *each*) cream
        cheese
    1 tablespoon sesame seed
    1 tablespoon soy sauce (optional)
    2 tablespoons chopped fresh
        chives
    2 to 3 tablespoons taco sauce

Cream cheese blocks should be left whole and brought to room temperature. Toast sesame seed by spreading in a shallow baking pan or on a cooky sheet and placing in a 350° oven for about 5 minutes or until golden.

Coat 1 block of cheese with sesame seed and place on tray; for added zest, drizzle soy sauce over top. Press chives into second cheese block to cover all of the surface generously. Place third cheese block on tray and spoon over it about half of taco sauce; add more sauce as required. Makes 12 servings.

Fresh Creamy Cheese (page 19).

Nut-studded Appetizer Cheeses
(counter-clockwise from left):
herbed cheese with sliced almonds,
herbed cheese with pine nuts,
Camembert with slivered almonds.
(Recipes on page 22)

NUT-STUDDED APPETIZER CHEESES

(Pictured on page 21)

The European custom of ending a meal with a bit of cheese and a few crunchy nuts is too good an idea to leave alone. The French have already taken it one elegant step further: often they present cheeses attractively studded with nuts.

Instead of offering this zestful cheese-and-nut combination just for dessert, why not serve it with raw vegetables or crisp crackers and present it as an appetizer?

Try combining flavors and textures. Lay crisp walnut halves on a wedge of creamy Oregon blue cheese, or pierce the rind of pungent Camembert or Brie with a bristle of almonds. You can flavor cream cheese, shape it, and give it a golden pine nut coating.

Since nuts tend to lose their crispness by absorbing moisture from the cheese, we recommend assembling the following recipes no more than a few hours before serving. If you make one of the flavored cream cheeses, though, you can shape it as much as a day ahead and add the nuts later.

Some recipes call for nuts you buy salted and roasted; others specify toasted nuts. To toast nuts, spread them in a single layer in a shallow baking pan. Bake, uncovered, in a 350° oven, shaking pan occasionally, for about 12 to 15 minutes or until nuts are golden brown (time varies with the size of the nut).

Allow about 1 ounce of cheese per serving and ¼ to ⅓ cup nuts to coat each 3 to 4 ounces of cheese.

Schloss or Blue Cheese with Walnuts. Bring to room temperature a piece of medium-ripe schloss or a wedge of creamy blue-veined cheese, such as Oregon blue or Gorgonzola (trim any rind off Gorgonzola). Press walnut halves firmly into top and sides of cheese. Serve with celery stalks, zucchini slices, and crackers.

Camembert or Brie with Almonds. Stud top and sides of a piece of medium-ripe Camembert or Brie with toasted slivered almonds or almond halves embedded on end. Serve with cauliflowerets, celery or carrot sticks, and crackers.

Teleme or Breakfast Cheese with Salted Nuts. Let a chunk of teleme or a round of medium-ripe breakfast cheese come to room temperature. Press salted almonds or pecans into top and sides, or stud surface with nuts embedded on end. Serve with carrot sticks, jícama slices, red or green pepper strips, and salted crackers.

Herbed Cheese with Nuts. Press toasted pine nuts or almond halves into herb-flavored cheeses, such as boursin, rondelé, or Gervais.

Or beat together until blended 1 small package (3 oz.) cream cheese or Neufchâtel (at room temperature), 2 large cloves garlic (minced or pressed), 1 teaspoon fine herbes (or ¼ teaspoon *each* crumbled thyme and oregano leaves and ⅛ teaspoon *each* rubbed sage, crumbled marjoram leaves, dry rosemary, and dry basil), and ¼ teaspoon salt.

Wrap with clear plastic film, shape, and chill; then unwrap and cover with toasted pine nuts or slivered almonds. Serve with radishes, green pepper strips, zucchini slices, and crackers.

Shallot Cream Cheese with Nuts. Beat together until blended 1 small package (3 oz.) chive cream cheese (at room temperature), ¼ teaspoon salt, and 1 tablespoon finely chopped shallots. Wrap with clear plastic film, shape, and chill; then unwrap and cover with toasted pine nuts or slivered almonds. Serve with cherry tomatoes, cucumber slices, radishes, and crackers.

Cherry Cheese with Almonds. Stud top and sides of a wedge of cherry cheese, such as gourmandise or Nec Plus Ultra, with toasted almond halves embedded on end. Serve with plain crackers.

FREEZER CHEESE BALLS

Your freezer can be your ally when you make these cheese balls ahead for a party or to have on hand for last-minute entertaining.

- 2 cups (8 oz.) shredded sharp Cheddar cheese
- 1 large package (8 oz.) cream cheese or Neufchâtel
- 4 ounces blue cheese, cut into pieces
- ¼ cup butter or margarine
- 1 clove garlic, minced or pressed
- ⅔ cup coarsely chopped walnuts or pecans

Allow cheeses and butter to stand at room temperature until soft. Shred or cut Cheddar into small pieces and put into the large bowl of an electric mixer. Add cream cheese, blue cheese, and butter; beat until blended. Add garlic and beat until creamy.

Cover and chill cheese mixture for about 3 hours or until firm enough to shape into balls. Divide in half and shape each half into a smooth ball; wrap airtight in clear plastic film, place in a plastic bag, and refrigerate or freeze until needed.

Allow frozen cheese balls to stand at room temperature, unwrapped, 3 or 4 hours before serving. Sprinkle nuts on a piece of wax paper and roll each ball in about ⅓ cup of the nuts, pressing in lightly. Serve with assorted crackers or wafers. Makes 2 balls, each about 3 inches in diameter.

ALMOND-CHEDDAR BALL

Pickles and Sherry, a pair of unlikely ingredients, flavor this cheese ball studded with almonds.

- 4 cups (1 lb.) shredded sharp Cheddar cheese
- 1 large package (8 oz.) cream cheese, softened
- ⅓ cup finely chopped sweet pickle
- 2 tablespoons *each* dry Sherry and mayonnaise
- 1 tablespoon Dijon mustard
  Dash cayenne
- ¾ cup coarsely chopped almonds

Beat Cheddar cheese and cream cheese together until smoothly blended. Add pickle, Sherry, mayonnaise, mustard, and cayenne; mix well. Cover and chill until firm enough to handle.

Spread almonds in a baking pan and toast in a 350° oven for 8 minutes or until evenly browned.

Divide cheese mixture in half and shape each half into a ball. Wrap airtight and refrigerate at least 2 hours—or as long as 2 weeks. Before serving, roll in almonds to coat evenly and let stand at room temperature about ½ hour. Serve with crackers. Makes 2 balls, each about 4 inches in diameter.

STUFFED GOUDA CHEESE

A hollowed-out baby Gouda cheese, its contents whipped with butter and seasonings, can be attractively featured on a cheese tray. This spread goes nicely with thin pumpernickel slices.

- 1 baby Gouda cheese (14-oz. size)
- ½ cup beer
- 1 teaspoon prepared Dijon mustard
- ⅛ teaspoon ground nutmeg
- ¼ cup butter or margarine, softened and cut in chunks
- ½ teaspoon caraway seed

Cut out a circle from center of top of cheese. Carefully scoop out cheese inside, leaving shell intact. Use a curved small knife, such as a grapefruit knife, to remove cheese at first; finish the job carefully with a spoon to avoid puncturing shell.

Place ¼ cup of the beer in a blender. Cut larger pieces of cheese into cubes; add all the cheese to blender with mustard, nutmeg, and butter. Whirl until smooth, adding remaining beer gradually with motor running; stir down with spatula occasionally. Stir in caraway seed. Spoon cheese mixture into shell; refill later with remainder. Cheese mixture can be refrigerated until next day. Makes about 1½ cups.

CARAWAY ROLL

Though just right for spreading, the mixture for this roll can be thinned with additional cream or beer and beaten to become a dip.

- 1 large package (8 oz.) cream cheese, softened
- ⅓ cup whipping cream or beer
- 3 cups (12 oz.) shredded jack cheese
- 1 tablespoon caraway seed
  About 1 teaspoon seasoned salt
- ⅓ cup shredded Parmesan cheese

Blend cream cheese with cream or beer, then beat until fluffy. Add jack cheese, caraway seed, and seasoned salt, adding more salt to taste if desired. Mix well and spoon onto foil or wax paper that has been sprinkled with the Parmesan cheese. Shape into a log, coating the outside with shredded cheese. (If mixture is too soft to handle, chill a short time until you can shape it.) Chill log until firm, 2 hours or more. Makes about 12 servings.

GARLIC-HERB CHEESE

Reminiscent of French *boursin*, this cheese spread is spiced with savory and garlic. Fresh bulk cream cheese from a delicatessen or cheese shop will make the tastiest spread.

- ½ pound cream cheese, softened
- 3 tablespoons lemon juice
- ½ teaspoon dried or 1 teaspoon fresh winter or summer savory
- ¼ to ½ teaspoon freshly ground black pepper
- 1 clove garlic, minced or pressed
  Whipping cream or milk

Beat cream cheese until smooth. Beat in lemon juice, savory, pepper, and garlic. If mixture seems too thick, add a little cream. Mound in a small serving bowl or press into a greased mold; or wrap with clear plastic film, then shape and chill as directed in Nut-studded Appetizer Cheeses (page 22). Makes about 1¼ cups.

Creamy Parmesan Fondue (page 25).

Creamy raclette melts before a toasty
fire. Serve with tiny new potatoes and
marinated onions. (Recipe on page 26)

fondues

MEAT AND SEAFOOD FONDUE APPETIZER

Oil fondues are a good choice for party appetizers because all the preparation can be done ahead, and guests do their own cooking.

There are two essentials to serving an oil fondue: a good cooking unit that will keep the oil hot, yet be safe to use at the table; and a good cut of meat or fish. You can serve several types of meat or fish at the same time, but *don't cook fish and meat in the same oil.*

Select a variety of sauces to accompany the fondue. Following are four sauce recipes, all of which can be served with either meat or fish, as well as suggestions for several sauces that can be purchased ready-made.

Salad Oil
Boneless beef sirloin or tenderloin, well trimmed and cut in bite-size pieces; *or* boneless leg of lamb, well trimmed and cut in bite-size pieces; *or* raw scallops, cut in half; *or* raw prawns, shelled and deveined; *or* boneless salmon, trimmed and cut in bite-size pieces (allow ⅛ to ¼ pound boneless meat or fish per person)
Salt and pepper
Sauces (recipes and purchasing suggestions follow)

Fill a fondue pot ⅓ to ½ full with oil; set over low heat and slowly heat to 375° on a deep-fat-frying thermometer (or use electric fondue pot following manufacturer's instructions). Carefully transfer pot of hot oil to serving table and place over heating unit; adjust heat to keep oil at correct temperature. Arrange tray of meat or fish, salt and pepper, and condiment sauces alongside fondue pot.

Guests spear 1 or 2 pieces of meat or fish at a time on fondue forks and immerse them in hot oil until cooked as desired—allow about 30 seconds for medium-rare meat; allow fish to take on a tinge of brown on its edges (about 1 minute).

After cooking, guests transfer cubes of meat or fish to a plate, season lightly with salt and pepper, and, with a regular fork, dip into desired sauce.

Mock Béarnaise Sauce. In a blender, put 1 teaspoon tarragon and 1 tablespoon tarragon vinegar; let stand 2 minutes. Add 1 cup mayonnaise, ⅛ teaspoon dry mustard, and 2 tablespoons finely minced shallots or green onion (white part only); whirl until smoothly blended. Cover and chill until next day, if desired. Makes about 1¼ cups.

Spicy Chile Sauce. In a small pan, stir together ¾ cup tomato-based chile sauce, ½ cup finely chopped onion, 3 tablespoons lemon juice, 2 tablespoons salad oil, 2 teaspoons tarragon vinegar, 1 clove garlic (minced or pressed), 1 teaspoon brown sugar, ½ teaspoon liquid hot pepper seasoning, and ¼ teaspoon *each* salt and dry mustard until well blended. Bring to boiling over high heat; reduce heat to low and simmer until onion is slightly limp and sauce is thickened (about 5 minutes).

Serve hot or at room temperature. If desired, cover and chill as long as 2 days. To reheat, place sauce in a small pan and bring to boiling over high heat. Makes 1¼ cups.

Curried Chutney Sauce. In a small bowl, stir together ¾ cup unflavored yogurt *or* sour cream, 1 teaspoon curry powder, and ¼ cup finely chopped Major Grey chutney until well blended. Cover and chill until next day, if desired. Makes about 1 cup.

Teriyaki Sauce. In a small pan, stir together 1 tablespoon cornstarch and 2 teaspoons *each* lemon juice and dry Sherry until smoothly blended. Gradually stir in until well blended 1 chicken bouillon cube dissolved in ¾ cup hot water, 3 tablespoons soy sauce, 1 tablespoon honey, 1 clove garlic (minced or pressed), and 1 teaspoon finely shredded fresh ginger *or* ½ teaspoon ground ginger. Cook, stirring, over high heat until sauce boils, thickens, and clears.

Serve hot or at room temperature. If desired, cover and chill as long as 2 days. To reheat, place sauce in a small pan and bring to boiling over high heat. Makes about 1 cup.

Purchased Sauces for Fish Fondue. Prepared tartar sauce, bottled cocktail sauce, or canned sweet and sour sauce.

Purchased Sauces for Beef or Lamb Fondue. Canned avocado dip; thick, bottled, cream-based blue cheese or green goddess dressing; or canned hollandaise.

CREAMY PARMESAN FONDUE

(Pictured on opposite page)

Almost indestructible, this fondue can be made ahead and reheated to serve a sizeable group.

> 2 large packages (8 oz. *each*) cream cheese or Neufchâtel
> About 2 cups milk
> 2 small cloves garlic, minced or pressed (or 1 teaspoon garlic salt)
> About 1½ cups shredded or grated Parmesan cheese
> Salt
> Freshly ground pepper or thin slices of green onion
> About 1-pound loaf French bread, cut in 1-inch cubes

Put cream cheese into the top of a double boiler and set over simmering water. As cheese melts, gradually stir in milk until mixture blends into a smooth sauce. Add garlic and Parmesan; stir until cheese melts and thickens the sauce. Add salt to taste and more milk if needed to thin to good dipping consistency.

Serve in a chafing dish over hot water or in a ceramic cheese fondue pot over a low alcohol flame. Sprinkle with fresh pepper or green onion. Serve with bread cubes and fondue forks or long wooden skewers for dipping. Makes about 1 quart fondue (12 to 16 servings).

EASY, NEVER-FAIL FONDUES

If you want to serve something out of the ordinary, try one of these two different approaches to fondue. Neither has the traditional base of shredded cheese. The first recipe, Italian-style Fondue, is a robust tomato sauce, thick with Cheddar and Parmesan. Make your favorite meatballs or sausage balls to spear and dunk in the sauce. Try it, too, with vegetables (such as cooked whole artichokes and lightly cooked whole carrots, green beans, or broccoli) or with bread sticks or cubes of crusty French bread.

The second never-fail recipe, Chiles-in-Cheese Fondue, is based on canned white sauce and jack cheese. It can easily be transported to the patio or to a picnic. Serve it with canned Vienna sausages (or frankfurters roasted over a picnic fire), crisp-fried tortillas (page 15), or raw vegetables.

Italian-style Fondue

- 2 tablespoons butter or margarine
- 1 medium-size onion, finely chopped
- 1 clove garlic, minced or pressed
- 1 small can (about 8 oz.) stewed tomatoes
- ½ teaspoon basil leaves
- ¼ teaspoon oregano leaves
- ⅛ teaspoon pepper
- 2 cups (8 oz.) shredded Longhorn Cheddar cheese
- ¼ cup shredded Parmesan cheese
- 1 tablespoon cornstarch
- 1 tablespoon dry Sherry (optional)
- Half-and-half (light cream) or milk

In a frying pan, melt butter; add onion and garlic and cook, stirring, until onion is golden. Stir in tomatoes, basil, oregano, and pepper. Heat to simmering, mashing tomatoes with a fork. Meanwhile combine Longhorn cheese with Parmesan cheese and cornstarch.

Reduce heat to a gentle simmer and add cheese mixture, a handful at a time, stirring until melted and blended. Stir in Sherry. Mix in a little half-and-half if needed to thin for dipping. Transfer to fondue pot Makes about 2 cups (8 appetizer servings).

Chiles-in-Cheese Fondue

- 1 can (10½ oz.) white sauce
- ½ to 1 can (4 oz.) California green chiles, seeded and chopped
- 1 clove garlic, minced or pressed (or garlic salt to taste)
- 3 cups (12 oz.) shredded jack cheese
- Milk or white wine

Turn white sauce into a pan and add chiles and garlic. Heat, stirring, until mixture comes to a boil. Lower heat and gradually mix in cheese; stir until melted and smooth. Stir in a little milk or white wine if needed to thin for dipping. Transfer to fondue pot over heat source. Makes about 2 cups (8 appetizer servings).

RACLETTE

(Pictured on page 24)

The staging of *raclette* is unusual and almost as inviting as the taste. You place a chunk of cheese in front of the hearth fire. As the face of the cheese close to the heat begins to melt and flow, it is quickly scraped off, spooned onto a bite of boiled potato, and then garnished with marinated onions and pickles.

Adjust quantities so raclette will be used on one occasion.

- 2 to 3-pound chunk mellow flavor cheese, such as jack, fontina, Gruyère, Samsoe, Swiss, or Swiss-made raclette (avoid cheese that strings excessively, like mozzarella)
- Boiled potatoes (directions follow)
- Marinated onions (directions follow)
- About 2 cups small sweet pickles

Place cheese, trimmed of any wax, in a shallow pan somewhat larger than cheese chunk. Set pan on hearth and push wide surface of cheese in close to fire.

When cheese face begins to melt, scrape it off and spoon onto a bite of hot potato with marinated onions (directions for both follow) and sweet pickles.

Pull cheese away from heat until you are ready for next serving; each person can tend to his or her own needs.

If you have no fireplace, use your broiler. Arrange ½-inch-thick slices side by side to cover the bottom of a shallow pan (such as a pie pan). Broil about 4 inches from heat until melted and bubbling; serve at once. Have ready as many pans of cheese as you will need, and broil when ready to serve. Makes about 20 servings.

Boiled Potatoes. Scrub 3 pounds very small new potatoes and boil in water to cover until tender when pierced (about 20 minutes). Drain off most of the water and cut potatoes into slices, if desired. Set potatoes, covered, next to fire to keep warm.

Marinated Onions. Thinly slice 2 medium-size mild white onions. Mix with ⅓ cup white wine vinegar, ½ teaspoon salt, and 1½ teaspoons sugar. Cover and chill at least 1 hour; mix occasionally.

FONDUTA

The elegant cheese sauce of northern Italy—*fonduta*—is best known served like the grand Swiss fondue—in a communally shared container with chunks of bread for dipping.

But fonduta is considerably more versatile. Less rich and easier to make than fondue, it is basically a custard into which fontina cheese is melted. The sauce can be made ahead and rewarmed. We're presenting fonduta as an appetizer; it is equally good as a sauce for pasta, vegetables, meats, or eggs.

Traditionally and extravagantly, a final addition to the sauce is the aromatic white truffle, cut in paper-thin slivers.

- 4 egg yolks
- 1 cup milk
- 3 cups (about 12 oz.) finely shredded fontina cheese
- 1 can (½ oz.) white truffles (optional)
  About ½ of a 1-pound loaf French bread, cut in 1-inch cubes

In the top of a double boiler, blend egg yolks well with milk. Place over simmering water (water should just touch bottom of top unit). Cook, stirring constantly with a flexible spatula, for 7 to 8 minutes or until mixture is thickened enough to coat a metal spoon with a thick, velvety layer (if overcooked, custard mixture looks grainy, then separates).

Stir in cheese immediately and continue to cook, stirring, until all but a few slivers of cheese are smoothly melted. Remove double boiler from heat but leave fonduta sauce over hot water for about 10 minutes, stirring occasionally. (At this point you can cover and chill fonduta for as long as 5 days. To reheat, place desired quantity over simmering water, stirring until warm enough to serve.)

If truffles are used, drain their juice into fonduta. Cut truffles into paper-thin slices and stir most of the slices into sauce. Reserve a few to sprinkle on as garnish when fonduta is used as a sauce. Makes about 2½ cups sauce.

To serve, pour warm fonduta into top unit of a chafing dish and set over hot water; keep warm. Dip cubes of crusty bread into sauce.

CLASSIC SWISS FONDUE

A pot of bubbling Swiss cheese fondue makes a fine party appetizer—elegant to serve, yet informal in style.

Make and serve your Swiss fondue in any of the pots made especially for cheese fondue. They are of heavy, heat-resistant earthenware or heavy metal which, when used over a controllable heat unit, maintains the low, even heat that is important for melting cheese into a smooth sauce.

Your heat source should maintain a temperature that will keep the cheese at the simmering point. If the cheese mixture gets too cool, it becomes tough; if it becomes too hot, it gets stringy.

Should the fondue become too thick, add a small amount of warmed—never cold—wine and stir in completely.

- 1 clove garlic, cut in half
- 2 cups light dry white wine (such as Riesling, Chablis, or Traminer)
- ½ pound imported Swiss cheese (Emmenthaler), shredded or diced
- ½ pound Swiss Gruyère or Danish Samsoe, shredded or diced
- 1 tablespoon cornstarch
- 1 teaspoon dry mustard (optional)
- 3 tablespoons kirsch (optional)
  Freshly ground nutmeg and pepper
- 1 small loaf French bread, cut in bite-size cubes and with some crust on each

Rub sides and bottom of fondue pot with garlic. Add wine; place over high heat until bubbles form and rise to surface. Reduce heat to simmering. In a bowl, combine cheeses, cornstarch, and mustard. Add cheese mixture, a spoonful at a time, to simmering wine; stir slowly and continuously until cheese is blended into a smooth sauce—it should bubble very slowly.

Stir in kirsch, a tablespoon at a time, and again bring to a simmer. (If heat gets too high at any time, fondue may separate.) Sprinkle with nutmeg and pepper to taste. Take to table, along with bread cubes, and adjust heat so fondue keeps bubbling slowly. With fondue forks, guests swirl bread cubes through cheese in a figure-8 pattern.

Makes about 2½ cups or enough for 12 appetizer servings.

Hot Appetizers
from the stove, the oven, or the barbecue

*H*ors d'oeuvres piping hot from the oven are always popular party treats. They can be as simple to make as Parmesan Pocket Bread Appetizers or Hasty Hots—or as elaborate as some of the filled pastries shown on the opposite page.

The pastry chef will be intrigued with the many recipes dealing with familiar pastries in miniature. In addition to recipes for Mini-Bagels, Cocktail Cream Puffs, mini-pizzas, and Cocktail Baking Powder Biscuits, you'll find recipes for tarts, quiches, and crackers flavored with cheese, shrimp, beef, or sesame seed.

Hot appetizers that beg to be tried include an abundance of vegetable, meat, and seafood recipes, such as stuffed mushrooms and crunchy artichokes, savory meatballs, garlicky snails, and spicy prawns. All should be served hot, but many can be prepared in advance and reheated just before serving.

For a change of pace, try hors d'oeuvres from the barbecue. Succulent smoked salmon with a glossy syrup and spice glaze can be made easily in a covered barbecue, with smoldering coals and smoky hickory chips. Your barbecue can also double as cooker and server for the hot-off-the-grill appetizers.

Many of the hot appetizers reflect foreign influences. From Mexico and from Central and South America come Appetizer Turnovers, Queso al Horno, Tostadas de Harina, and Spanish Picadillo Pastries. Cheese-filled Diamonds and Meat-filled Fila Triangles are Greek in origin; Quiche Lorraine Appetizer hails from France.

Favorite ethnic dishes, borrowed for appetizers and bearing such colorful names as Rumaki, Falafil, Samosas, Lumpia Appetizer, and Chinese Won Ton, add variety to any hors d'oeuvre presentation.

Hot pastry appetizers (counter-clockwise from upper left): Shrimp Quiches, Cheese-filled Diamonds, Appetizer Turnovers, Quiche Lorraine Appetizer, Cheese & Seed Nibbles, Cheese & Caraway Appetizers, Quick Pastry Twists, and Picadillo Pastries. (Recipes on pages 30–35)

SHRIMP QUICHES

(Pictured on page 29)

These two-bite quiches, baked in small-cup muffin pans, use refrigerator rolls for their crusts.

    1 package (8 oz.) refrigerated but-
      terflake dinner rolls
      About ¾ cup (4 oz.) small
      cooked shrimp
    1 egg
    ½ cup whipping cream or half-
      and-half (light cream)
    2 tablespoons finely minced green
      onion
    ½ teaspoon salt
    ¼ teaspoon dill weed
    ⅛ teaspoon cayenne
    ½ cup shredded Swiss cheese

Generously grease 2 dozen 1¾-inch muffin cups; set aside.

Separate rolls into 12 equal pieces. Cut each in half; press each half into bottom and sides of a muffin cup. Divide shrimp evenly among pastry shells.

Beat together egg, cream, onion, salt, dill, and cayenne until well blended. Using about 2 teaspoons for each, divide evenly among shells; sprinkle cheese over tops. Bake, uncovered, in a 375° oven for 20 minutes or until edges are brown and centers appear set. Cool 5 minutes to serve warm.

Or remove from muffin pans and cool completely on racks; then package airtight and freeze. To reheat, place frozen quiches on a baking sheet; bake in a 375° oven for 15 minutes or until heated throughout. Makes 24 appetizers.

QUICHE LORRAINE APPETIZER

(Pictured on page 29)

The method for making this French-style appetizer is simple. You bake the rich crust "blind" (empty) in a large baking pan until golden, then pour the filling into the crust and bake it again. Though quite delicate, this quiche cuts and serves neatly for a hot appetizer.

    14 strips (about ¾ lb.) bacon
    1¼ cups (6 oz.) shredded Swiss
       cheese
       Baked pastry shell (recipe fol-
       lows)
     4 eggs
    1¼ cups whipping cream
     ½ cup milk
       Fresh grated nutmeg (or ground
       nutmeg)

Cook bacon until crisp; cool, then crumble. Evenly distribute bacon and cheese over bottom of baked pastry shell. Lightly beat eggs; add cream and milk and beat until well blended. Pour egg mixture over cheese and bacon. Sprinkle a little nutmeg over filling.

Bake, uncovered, in a 325° oven for 25 minutes or until filling appears set when gently shaken (if it puffs, prick with a fork to allow air to escape). Cut in small squares and serve hot or at room temperature on napkins or little plates. Makes 40 pieces about 2 inches square.

Pastry Shell. Measure 1½ cups unsifted all-purpose flour into a bowl. Add ⅛ teaspoon salt and 9 tablespoons (½ cup plus 1 table-

spoon) butter or margarine, cut in small pieces. With a pastry blender or your fingers, break butter into very small particles; the largest should be the size of small peas. Beat 1 egg and add to flour mixture, blending well with a fork. Shape mixture with your hands to form a compact ball.

On a well-floured board, roll dough to fit a 10 by 15-inch shallow-rimmed baking pan; turn dough occasionally to prevent sticking. Gently fit pastry flush with top edge of pan and trim evenly if necessary. (If it tears, just press broken edges together.) Prick bottom with a fork.

Bake, uncovered, in a 425° oven for 12 to 15 minutes or until lightly browned. Cool. Wrap airtight if crust will not be used within an hour or two.

CHEDDAR TARTS

For an unusual appetizer, serve these bite-size pies warm from the oven or at room temperature.

      Pastry for a single-crust 9-inch
      pie
    ½ cup fine fresh bread crumbs
    2 eggs, well beaten
    2 tablespoons butter or margarine,
      softened
    ½ cup shredded sharp Cheddar
      cheese
    ⅓ cup milk
    ¼ teaspoon liquid hot pepper sea-
      soning
    ¼ teaspoon salt
      Dash of pepper
    1 teaspoon baking powder

Prepare your own pastry or use a pie crust mix. Roll out dough on a lightly floured board into about a 12-inch circle. With a 3-inch cooky cutter, cut dough into rounds. Using a muffin pan whose cups are 1¾ inches in diameter, press and fit each round into bottom and sides of muffin cups. Continue to reroll and cut pastry scraps to make a total of 15 to 18 tart shells.

Mix together crumbs, eggs, butter, cheese, milk, hot pepper seasoning, salt, pepper, and baking

powder. Fill each tart shell with about 1 tablespoon cheese mixture. Bake, uncovered, in a 400° oven for 25 minutes or until top is set when lightly tapped. Serve warm or cooled. Makes 15 to 18 appetizer tarts.

CHEESE-FILLED DIAMONDS

(Pictured on page 29)

These Greek-style appetizers called *bourekakia* are filled with a mild cheese mixture. Purchase ready-made fila dough at international delicatessens or in the frozen food section of markets that carry gourmet foods.

  1 large package (8 oz.) cream cheese
½ pound feta cheese
  2 cups large curd cottage cheese
  3 egg yolks
  2 tablespoons minced parsley
  1 cup (½ lb.) butter or margarine
    About 24 sheets fila dough (about ⅔ of a 1-lb. package)

Beat together cream cheese, feta cheese, cottage cheese, egg yolks, and parsley until well blended and creamy.

Melt butter in a small pan; set aside. Lay out 3 sheets of fila (keep remaining fila covered with clear plastic film). Lightly brush 1 sheet with butter, using a wide pastry brush; lay on another sheet, lightly brush with butter; top with third sheet, lightly brush with butter.

Spoon a ½-inch-wide ribbon of cheese mixture along 1 long side of dough. Starting from that side, roll up jelly-roll fashion, tucking in ends as you work to encase filling. Place seam side down on an ungreased baking sheet. Repeat, making 7 more rolls and placing them about 1 inch apart (you'll need 2 baking sheets).

Bake, uncovered, in a 375° oven for 15 minutes or until puffed and lightly browned. Let cool 15 minutes; then slice through each roll on the diagonal about 2¼ inches apart, making diamond-shaped pieces. Serve at once.

Or cool completely, cover, and chill until next day; for longer storage, wrap airtight and freeze. To reheat (thaw if frozen), bake, uncovered, in a 375° oven for 15 minutes or until brown and puffy. Makes 4 dozen appetizers.

CHEESE SPRITZ

A spritz cooky press shapes the dough best in this recipe. Try Christmas shapes for the holidays, simple shapes for other occasions.

  ⅔ cup butter or margarine, softened
  ½ cup shredded sharp Cheddar cheese
  2 egg yolks
  ⅛ teaspoon cayenne
  ¼ teaspoon dry mustard
  ½ teaspoon *each* salt and sugar
1¾ cup sifted all-purpose flour
    Poppy seed, sesame seed, or pimento

In bowl of electric mixer, beat together butter and cheese. Add egg yolks, cayenne, mustard, salt, and sugar; beat until well blended. Add flour and stir until smoothly blended. Form dough into a ball. Put part of dough at a time into a spritz cooky press and shape cookies on baking sheets. Or chill dough 1 hour, roll on floured board, cut with fancy cooky cutters, and place on baking sheets. Decorate with poppy seed, sesame seed, or pimento. Bake, uncovered, in a 375° oven for about 12 minutes or until lightly browned. Serve warm or cooled. Makes 3 dozen appetizers.

PUFFY CHEESE APPETIZERS

Frozen patty shells make the base for these hot and tasty pastries.

  1 package (10 oz.) frozen patty shells
  1 egg, lightly beaten
  1 tablespoon sesame seed
  1 tablespoon butter or margarine
  ½ cup finely chopped onion
  ¼ cup finely chopped parsley
  ½ teaspoon salt
    Dash *each* cayenne and ground allspice
  2 cups (8 oz.) coarsely shredded jack cheese

Allow patty shells to thaw just until pliable (about 30 minutes). On a lightly floured board, arrange 2 rows of 3 shells each so shells all overlap slightly. Roll and pat into a rectangle about 10 by 15 inches. Carefully transfer to a 10 by 15-inch shallow-rimmed baking pan; prick bottom with a fork. Brush egg over surface and sprinkle with sesame seed. Bake, uncovered, in a 450° oven for 15 minutes.

Meanwhile melt butter in a small pan over medium heat; add onion and cook until limp. Add parsley, salt, cayenne, and allspice; cook for 1 minute. Remove from heat and stir in cheese.

Remove pastry from oven and spoon cheese mixture to within ½ inch of edges. Return to oven and bake, uncovered, until cheese is melted and pastry is well browned (about 5 minutes). Cut into 2-inch squares and serve hot. Makes about 28 appetizers.

Hors d'oeuvres by candlelight: Glazed Sausage Balls and Crab-stuffed Mushrooms. (Recipes on pages 39, 43)

CHEESE STRAWS

These crisp little strips of cheese pastry make elegant party hors d'oeuvres.

- ½ teaspoon *each* salt and powdered ginger
- 1 cup sifted all-purpose flour
- ⅓ cup butter or margarine
- 1 cup (about 4 oz.) shredded sharp Cheddar cheese
- ¼ cup sesame seed, toasted
- ½ teaspoon Worcestershire
- 2 to 2½ tablespoons cold water

Sift together salt, ginger, and flour. Cut in butter with a pastry blender as you would for pastry. Lightly stir in cheese and sesame seed. Add Worcestershire to 1 tablespoon of the water, sprinkle over flour, and toss with a fork. Add remaining water while tossing mixture with a fork until moistened. Gather up with fingers and form into a ball.

On a lightly floured board, roll out ⅛ inch thick. Cut with a pastry wheel or knife into strips about 3 inches long and ½ inch wide.

Place about 1 inch apart on ungreased baking sheets and bake, uncovered, in a 400° oven for about 10 to 12 minutes or until lightly browned and crisp. Makes 6 to 7 dozen appetizers.

SESAME CHEESE WAFERS

Sesame seed coats a cheese log that can be prepared in advance and then refrigerated or frozen. When you're ready, just slice into wafers and bake.

- 1 jar (5 oz.) sharp pasteurized process cheese spread
- ¼ cup butter or margarine, softened
- ⅔ cup all-purpose flour, unsifted
- 3 tablespoons sesame seed, toasted

In bowl of electric mixer, beat together cheese spread, butter, and flour until well blended.

Turn cheese mixture out onto a lightly floured board and shape into a smooth log 12 inches long.

Sprinkle board evenly with sesame seed; then roll log in seed, pressing lightly to embed seed around entire log. Wrap in wax paper and chill until firm or until next day. (Wrap airtight to freeze for longer storage.)

To bake (thaw if frozen), cut log into ¼-inch-thick slices and place 1 inch apart on ungreased baking sheets. Bake, uncovered, in a 375° oven for about 12 minutes or until wafers are golden on the bottom (turn one over to check). Transfer to a wire rack. Serve warm or cooled. Makes about 4 dozen wafers.

CHEESE AND SEED NIBBLES

(Pictured on page 29)

Divide the basic dough for these savory appetizers in half and make some with Parmesan and caraway seasoning, others with Cheddar cheese and poppy seeds.

- 3 tablespoons butter or margarine
- 2 cups biscuit mix (baking mix)
- ½ cup water
- 1 teaspoon caraway seed
- ½ cup grated Parmesan cheese
- 1 teaspoon poppy seed
- ½ cup shredded Cheddar cheese
- 1½ tablespoons cornmeal
- 4 tablespoons milk
- 15 pitted ripe olives
- 1½ tablespoons fine dry bread crumbs
- 15 pimento-stuffed olives

Cut butter into biscuit mix until mixture is like coarse cornmeal. Add water and stir until blended. Divide dough in half. To one half of dough, add caraway seed and ¼ cup of the Parmesan. To other half of dough, add poppy seed and ¼ cup of the Cheddar.

To shape Parmesan-caraway dough, combine remaining ¼ cup Parmesan and the cornmeal in a small bowl; put 2 tablespoons of the milk in another bowl; cut ripe olives in half. Form dough into 30 small balls; dip each in milk, then thoroughly coat with cheese-cornmeal mixture. Place 1½ inches apart on a well-greased

baking sheet; press half a ripe olive into top of each ball of dough to flatten slightly.

To shape Cheddar-poppy dough, combine the remaining ¼ cup Cheddar and bread crumbs in a small bowl; put 2 tablespoons of the milk in another bowl; cut pimento-stuffed olives in half. Form dough into 30 small balls; dip each in milk, then thoroughly coat with cheese-bread crumb mixture. Place 1½ inches apart on a well-greased baking sheet; press half a pimento-stuffed olive into top of each ball of dough to flatten slightly.

(At this point you may cover balls and leave at room temperature for an hour or two.)

Bake, uncovered, in a 375° oven for 10 to 15 minutes or until lightly browned. Serve hot. Makes 60 appetizers.

QUICK PASTRY TWISTS

(Pictured on page 29)

Puffy, flaky pastries can be quickly made from a packaged pie crust mix. Offer them warm from the oven or cooled.

- ½ cup shredded Cheddar cheese
- 1 package pie crust mix (enough for a single-crust 9-inch pie)
  Water
- 1 egg, beaten
  Caraway, poppy, or sesame seed, or coarse salt

Combine cheese with pie crust mix; add water and blend according to package directions. Turn out on a lightly floured board and roll into a 4 by 15-inch strip. Brush with egg and sprinkle evenly with caraway, poppy, or sesame seed, or coarse salt.

Cut across dough to make ½-inch-wide strips (each 4 inches long). Holding each strip at the ends, twist in opposite directions. Place about 1 inch apart on greased baking sheets and bake, uncovered, in a 400° oven for 10 minutes or until golden. Serve warm or cooled. Makes 2½ dozen pastry twists.

FREEZER CHEESE STICKS

A little effort with a loaf of frozen bread can reward you with a good supply of appetizers, ready to toast in the oven at any time.

- 1 loaf (1 lb.) white sandwich bread, unsliced
- 1 egg white
- ½ cup (¼ lb.) butter or margarine, softened
- 1 jar (5 oz.) pasteurized process sharp cheese spread, at room temperature

Place bread in freezer until frozen solid. Trim crusts from frozen bread with a long, sharp knife. Slice bread horizontally into 3 equal layers; cut each layer crosswise into ¾-inch strips.

Lightly beat egg white, add butter and cheese spread and beat until well blended and smooth. Spread on all sides of bread sticks. Place about 1 inch apart on greased baking sheets, cover with clear plastic film, and freeze until firm (at least 3 hours). Bake frozen sticks in a 325° oven for 15 to 20 minutes or until lightly browned. Serve piping hot. Makes about 4 dozen cheese sticks.

CHEESE AND CARAWAY APPETIZERS

(Pictured on page 29)

Made in the same manner as refrigerator cookies, these tender cheese pastries are convenient appetizers for any occasion. You refrigerate the rich dough shaped in a log; when you want freshly baked pastries, slice the dough, bake, and serve. If you want to start more than a few days in advance, freeze the dough and partially thaw before slicing.

- ¾ cup butter or margarine
- ½ cup shredded sharp Cheddar cheese
- ½ cup crumbled blue-veined cheese
- 2 cups all-purpose flour, unsifted
- 1½ teaspoons caraway seed
- 1 clove garlic, minced or pressed
- 2 tablespoons chopped chives (fresh, frozen, or freeze-dried)

In bowl of electric mixer, beat together butter, Cheddar cheese, and blue-veined cheese until smoothly blended. Stir in flour, caraway, garlic, and chives. Shape mixture into a log about 20 inches long and about 1¼ inches in diameter; wrap in wax paper and chill until firm or until next day. (Wrap airtight to freeze for longer storage.)

To bake (thaw if frozen), cut log into ¼-inch-thick slices and place 1 inch apart on ungreased baking sheets. Bake, uncovered, in a 375° oven for 10 to 12 minutes or until lightly browned around edges. Serve warm or cooled, plain or topped with a cherry tomato half or zucchini slice. Makes about 7 dozen wafers.

MEAT-FILLED TURNOVERS

A cottage cheese pastry forms the base for these small meat-filled turnovers. The dough goes together quickly and is easy to handle.

Making the turnovers takes some time, but you can prepare them in advance, freeze the baked pastries, and reheat as many as you wish before serving.

- 1 cup (½ lb.) butter or margarine, softened
- 1 cup small curd cottage cheese
- 2 cups all-purpose flour, unsifted
- ½ pound lean ground beef
- ½ teaspoon salt
- ⅓ cup chopped onion
- ¼ cup finely chopped mushrooms
- ¼ teaspoon dill weed
- ⅛ teaspoon pepper
- 3 tablespoons sour cream

Beat together butter and cottage cheese until well blended and creamy. Add flour and beat until thoroughly combined. Use immediately or cover and store in refrigerator for as long as 5 days. (If chilled, let dough come to room temperature before using.)

To make filling, crumble ground beef in a frying pan over medium heat; add salt and onion and cook, stirring, until beef is browned and onion is limp. Stir in mushrooms, dill weed, pepper, and sour cream. Blend well; set aside.

On a floured pastry cloth or board, roll out half the basic pastry dough at a time into a 10 by 16-inch rectangle (about ⅛ inch thick). Cut dough into 2-inch squares. Spoon about ¼ teaspoon of the filling onto one corner of each square; bring the opposite corner over the top to enclose filling. With a fork, press the open edges together to seal.

Place turnovers about 1 inch apart on ungreased baking sheets. Bake, uncovered, in a 350° oven for 15 to 18 minutes or until pastry is lightly browned. Serve warm.

Or cool completely on racks, wrap airtight, and freeze. To reheat, bake frozen pastries, uncovered, in a 350° oven for 10 minutes. Makes about 80 appetizers.

PICADILLO PASTRIES

(Pictured on page 29)

Spices and raisins flavor these *tapas* (Spanish-style appetizers). Pastry is wrapped around a savory meat mixture; then the stuffed "rings" are sliced and baked.

- 1 tablespoon butter or margarine
- 1 package (1¼ oz.) pine nuts
- 1 pound lean ground beef
- 1 onion, chopped
- 1 clove garlic, minced or pressed
- ½ cup raisins
- 1 teaspoon ground cinnamon
- ¼ teaspoon ground cloves
- ½ teaspoon salt
- ⅓ cup catsup
  Pastry for a double-crust 9-inch pie

Melt butter in a frying pan over medium heat. Add pine nuts and cook, stirring, until lightly toasted. Remove from pan and set aside.

Crumble ground beef in a frying pan over medium heat; add onion and garlic and cook, stirring, until meat is browned and onion is limp. Stir in raisins, cinnamon, cloves, salt, catsup, and

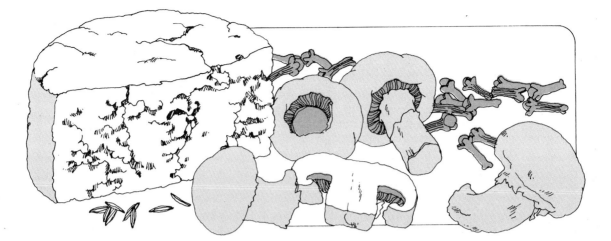

nuts. Heat, stirring, until hot throughout; set aside.

Meanwhile prepare pastry using your own recipe or a packaged pie crust mix. Divide dough in half. Roll each half into a 9 by 12-inch rectangle; spoon half the filling along one long side. Starting with that side, roll up jelly-roll fashion, moistening edge with water to seal. Tuck in ends and pinch to seal.

Cut across roll in 1-inch-thick slices and place cut side up on a lightly greased baking sheet. Repeat with remaining pastry and filling. Bake, uncovered, in a 350° oven for about 15 minutes or until lightly browned. Serve warm or cool. Makes 2 dozen pastries.

APPETIZER TURNOVERS

(Pictured on page 29)

Empanadillas, tiny South American turnovers, are easy to make at home with frozen patty shells and a choice of fillings.

Thaw 1 package (10 oz.) frozen patty shells (takes about 30 minutes). Slightly overlap them on a lightly floured board; roll out to $1/16$ to $1/8$-inch thickness. With a cooky cutter or empty tuna can (both ends removed), cut dough into $3^{1}/_{2}$-inch rounds.

Place a slightly rounded teaspoon of filling (recipes follow) on each round; fold in half, moisten edges with water, and press together with a fork to seal. Reroll pastry scraps and repeat filling procedure.

Place turnovers 1 inch apart on ungreased baking sheets. Prick tops with a fork and bake, uncovered, in a 400° oven for 20 minutes or until golden. Serve hot.

Or cool, wrap airtight, and freeze. To reheat, bake frozen turnovers, uncovered, in a 400° oven for 7 to 8 minutes. Makes about 2 dozen turnovers.

Spicy Beef Filling. Brown $1/2$ pound lean ground beef in a frying pan over medium heat. Add $1/4$ cup minced onion and cook until onion is limp; discard fat. Stir in 3 tablespoons *each* raisins, chopped ripe olives, and tomato-based chile sauce; 1 teaspoon chile powder; $1/2$ teaspoon *each* ground cumin, garlic salt, and ground coriander; add salt and pepper to taste.

Shrimp Filling. Combine $1/4$ pound small cooked shrimp (chopped), $1/4$ cup *each* chopped green onion and sweet pickle, 2 tablespoons finely chopped fresh coriander (cilantro), $1/4$ teaspoon *each* garlic salt and liquid hot pepper seasoning, 2 tablespoons sour cream, and salt and pepper to taste.

Chicken Filling. Combine $1/2$ cup finely chopped cooked chicken (about $1/2$ whole chicken breast), 1 can (4 oz.) California green chiles (seeded and chopped), $1/2$ cup shredded sharp Cheddar cheese, 3 tablespoons finely chopped almonds, and $1/2$ teaspoon *each* garlic salt and chile powder.

SALAMI AND CHEESE TURNOVERS

These filled pastries can be made ahead of time. That way they'll be ready to pop into the oven just before the party.

1 can (8 oz.) tomato sauce
1 cup (4 oz.) shredded jack cheese
1 cup finely chopped dry salami
$1/2$ teaspoon oregano leaves
$1/4$ teaspoon garlic powder
Enough pastry for 4 single-crust 9-inch pies

To make filling, in a bowl stir together tomato sauce, cheese, salami, oregano, and garlic powder until well blended; set aside.

Prepare pastry using your own recipe or a packaged mix. On a lightly floured board, roll out about $1/4$ of the pastry at a time until $1/8$ inch thick; cut into $2^{1}/_{2}$ to 3-inch rounds. Place about $3/4$ teaspoon filling off-center on each round; dampen edges with water, fold pastry in half, press edges together with a fork and prick tops. Place 2 inches apart on ungreased baking sheets and bake, uncovered, in a 450° oven for 10 minutes or until golden brown. Serve hot.

Or cool on wire racks, cover, and refrigerate until next day; for longer storage, wrap airtight and freeze. To reheat, bake, uncovered, in a 450° oven for 5 minutes (10 minutes if frozen) or until hot throughout. Makes 6 to 7 dozen turnovers.

WHEN THE PASTRY CHEF MAKES HORS D'OEUVRES

Individual servings of favorite breads—mini-pizzas, tiny bagels, bite-size cream puffs, and demi baking powder biscuits, served plain or filled with a spread or cheese—make very special hors d'oeuvres.

Another good choice for a dramatic pastry base is frozen puff pastry. You purchase frozen patty shells and roll them out to form one large piece of dough. Puffy Cheese Appetizers (page 31) and Appetizer Turnovers (page 35) both call for this easy-to-handle ingredient.

Pepperoni Pizza Appetizers

Regular-size pizzas, cut into bite-size squares, make dozens of hot hors d'oeuvres. This quick and easy version uses frozen bread dough for the crust and prepared pizza sauce for the topping. It can be made ahead and frozen for later use.

    1 loaf (1 lb.) frozen bread dough
      Olive oil or salad oil
    1 can (10 oz.) prepared pizza sauce
    1 teaspoon *each* dry basil and oregano
      leaves, crushed
    8 ounces pepperoni, thinly sliced
    ½ cup *each* minced green pepper and red
      onion
    2 cans (2¼ oz. *each*) sliced ripe olives,
      drained
    1 cup (about 3 oz.) freshly grated Parme-
      san cheese
    1 pound mozzarella cheese, coarsely
      shredded

Thaw dough according to package directions; divide in half. Grease two 10½ by 15½-inch jelly roll pans (or equivalent area of baking sheets) with oil.

On a lightly floured pastry cloth or wooden board, roll and stretch each dough half into a 9 by 14-inch rectangle. Transfer to pans, stretching to form a small ridge up pan sides. Lightly brush surface of dough with oil. Bake in a 500° oven 4 to 5 minutes or until crusts are lightly browned. Cool; cover and store at room temperature up to 1 day, if desired, or freeze for longer storage.

To top, stir together pizza sauce, basil, and oregano until blended. Evenly spread half the sauce mixture over each crust; top each with half the pepperoni. Place pepper, onion, and olives on paper towels to absorb any excess moisture; then sprinkle evenly over pepperoni. Top with Parmesan and mozzarella cheese.

Bake pizzas, one at a time, on lowest rack of a 500° oven for 8 to 10 minutes or until crust is richly browned and cheese is bubbly. Remove from oven and let sit until cool enough to handle. With scissors, cut into 2-inch squares. Serve warm. Makes about 72 appetizers.

Mini-Bagels

(Pictured on page 5)

Bite-size bagels make perfect hors d'oeuvre bases for creamy cheese spreads. A real luxury is to top the cream cheese with smoked salmon (recipe on page 44).

    2 cups warm (about 110°) water
    2 packages active dry yeast
    3 tablespoons sugar
    3 teaspoons salt
      About 5¾ cups all-purpose flour, un-
      sifted
    3 quarts water with 1 tablespoon sugar
      Cornmeal
    1 egg yolk beaten with 1 tablespoon
      water
      About 2 tablespoons poppy or sesame
      seed (optional)

Stir together water and yeast in large bowl of electric mixer; let stand 5 minutes to soften yeast. Stir in sugar and salt. Gradually mix in 4 cups of the flour and beat at medium speed for 5 minutes. With a spoon, stir in about 1¼ cups more flour to make a stiff dough.

Turn out on a floured board and knead until smooth, elastic, and no longer sticky (about 15 minutes); add more flour as needed to prevent sticking—dough should be firmer than

pan, cavity side up. Evenly mound filling in each mushroom cap, pressing it in firmly. (At this point you may cover and refrigerate until next day.)

To bake, sprinkle mushrooms with cheese and pour wine into pan. Bake, uncovered, in a 400° oven for 15 to 20 minutes or until hot throughout. Serve hot, garnished with parsley, on individual plates. Provide forks. Makes 3 dozen appetizers.

Crab-stuffed Mushrooms

- 24 (about 1¼ lb.) medium-size mushrooms
- 5 tablespoons butter or margarine
- 2 tablespoons minced green onion (use part of tops)
- 1 teaspoon lemon juice
- 1 cup (about 8 oz.) cooked fresh or canned crab meat
- ½ cup soft bread crumbs (about 1 slice firm white bread, whirled in blender)
- 1 egg, beaten
- ½ teaspoon dill weed
- ¾ cup shredded jack cheese
- ¼ cup dry white wine
  Lemon wedges (optional)

Remove stems from mushrooms; finely chop stems. Melt 2 tablespoons of the butter in a frying pan over medium heat. Add mushroom stems and onion and cook, stirring, until onion is limp. Remove from heat and stir in lemon juice, crab, bread crumbs, egg, dill weed, and ¼ cup of the cheese until well blended.

Melt remaining 3 tablespoons butter in a 9 by 13-inch baking pan. Turn mushroom caps in butter to coat. Place mushrooms in pan, cavity side up. Evenly mound filling in each mushroom cap, pressing it in firmly. (At this point you may cover and refrigerate until next day.)

To bake, sprinkle mushrooms with remaining cheese and pour wine into pan. Bake, uncovered, in a 400° oven for 15 to 20 minutes or until hot throughout. Serve hot (with lemon wedges to squeeze over, if desired) on individual plates. Provide forks. Makes 2 dozen appetizers.

HAPPY HOUR MUSHROOMS

(Pictured on page 4)

Don't let the name of this recipe fool you—these stuffed mushrooms are so good they won't last more than a few minutes.

- 10 (about ½ lb.) medium-size mushrooms
- 6 tablespoons butter or margarine, softened
- 1 clove garlic, minced or pressed
- 3 tablespoons shredded jack cheese
- 2 tablespoons dry white or red wine
- 1 teaspoon soy sauce
- ⅓ cup fine cracker crumbs

Remove stems from mushrooms and save for other uses. Melt 2 tablespoons of the butter; brush over mushroom caps, coating thoroughly. Stir together remaining 4 tablespoons butter, garlic, and cheese until well blended. Stir in wine, soy, and crumbs until well blended.

Place mushrooms, cavity side up, on a large rimmed baking sheet. Evenly mound filling in each mushroom, pressing it in lightly. Broil about 6 inches below broiler unit until bubbly and lightly browned (about 3 minutes). Serve warm. Makes about 10 appetizers.

PARMESAN-GARLIC ARTICHOKES

Greeting guests with tempting, hot hors d'oeuvres is easy for the cook who plans ahead. Made in advance, these artichokes topped with a cheesy garlic butter are ready to pop in the oven at party time.

- 1 package (9 oz.) frozen artichoke hearts
  About 2 dozen Melba toast rounds
- ¼ cup melted butter or margarine
- ¼ teaspoon garlic salt
  Dash of pepper
- 3 tablespoons Parmesan cheese

Cook artichoke hearts according to package directions. Drain well,

cut side down, on paper towels. Place each heart, cut side up, on a Melba toast round and place on a baking sheet.

Stir together butter, garlic salt, and pepper; drizzle evenly into crevices of artichokes and onto toast. Evenly sprinkle with cheese. (At this point you may cover and let stand at room temperature for as long as 6 hours.)

Bake, uncovered, in a 350° oven for 10 minutes or until hot. Makes about 2 dozen appetizers.

ARTICHOKE NIBBLES

These marinated artichoke hearts are baked in a spicy cheese and custard mixture and then cut in squares.

- 2 jars (6 oz. *each*) marinated artichoke hearts
- 1 small onion, finely chopped
- 1 clove garlic, minced or pressed
- 4 eggs
- ¼ cup fine dry bread crumbs
- ¼ teaspoon salt
- ⅛ teaspoon *each* pepper, oregano leaves, and liquid hot pepper seasoning
- 2 cups (8 oz.) shredded sharp Cheddar cheese
- 2 tablespoons minced parsley

Drain marinade from 1 jar of artichokes into a frying pan. Drain other jar (reserve marinade for other uses). Chop all artichokes; set aside. Heat marinade in frying pan over medium heat; add onion and garlic and cook, stirring, until onion is limp.

In a bowl, beat eggs with a fork. Stir in crumbs, salt, pepper, oregano, and hot pepper seasoning. Then stir in cheese, parsley, artichokes, and onion mixture. Turn into a greased 7 by 11-inch baking pan and bake, uncovered, in a 325° oven for about 30 minutes or until set when lightly touched. Let cool in pan, then cut into 1-inch squares. Serve warm or at room temperature.

Or cover, refrigerate, and serve cold. To reheat, bake, uncovered, in a 325° oven for 10 to 12 minutes or until hot. Makes about 6 dozen.

APPETIZERS FROM THE BARBECUE

Why not use your barbecue as a party prop next time you entertain? You can cook your hors d'oeuvres on it, then let guests serve themselves right from the grill at their own pace.

Italian-style Grilled Sausage and Cheese
(Pictured on page 53)

> About 1 pound mild Italian-style pork sausage
> About 1¼ pounds teleme (or mild jack) cheese
> About ¼ pound mozzarella cheese, shredded
> 1 loaf slender-shaped French bread, sliced, or about 6 French rolls, sliced

Cover sausage with water and bring to a boil; then reduce heat and simmer, covered, for 15 minutes. Drain and use hot or cold.

Cut teleme cheese into thick slices and spread over a 10 by 14-inch rimmed metal platter or pan. Sprinkle mozzarella over teleme.

To barbecue, arrange a small bed of coals equal to area of cheese pan. Ignite and when coals are hot, grill sausages 4 to 6 inches over coals until browned on all sides; push to a cool area of barbecue. Set cheese platter on grill directly over heat, place bread in a cooler area, and cover barbecue with hood or drape loosely with foil. When cheese is melted, push pan away from direct heat; slice a few sausages onto one end of pan.

Let guests serve themselves, making small sandwiches by topping French bread or roll slice with a spoonful of hot cheese and a piece of sausage. Makes 8 to 10 servings.

Pop-open Barbecue Clams
(Pictured on page 53)

Allow 6 to 8 clams for *each* serving; scrub in fresh water and arrange in a bowl.

To barbecue, ignite a bed of coals in a barbecue. Place clams, paper napkins, and a small fork for each person next to barbecue. Set grill 3 to 5 inches above coals. In a pan melt 1 tablespoon butter for *each* serving; push to a cool corner.

Each guest follows this procedure: set a clam on grill; after about 3 minutes, or when clam begins to open, turn it over and continue to cook until it pops wide open. Protecting fingers with a napkin, hold clam over butter pan to drain clam juices into butter. Then pluck out clam with fork, dip in butter, and eat. Leftover clam butter makes delicious dunking for bits of bread.

Barbecued Salmon with Biscuits

> 2½ to 3½-pound salmon fillet (half of a 5 to 7-lb. fish without head)
> ½ cup (¼ lb.) butter
> ¼ teaspoon grated lemon peel
> 2 tablespoons lemon juice
> Salt and pepper
> About 5 dozen Cocktail Baking Powder Biscuits (page 37)
> Watercress or curly endive (chicory)

Place fish, skin side down, on a double thickness of foil.

Melt butter in a small pan; add lemon peel and juice.

To barbecue, place just enough coals in barbecue to cover an area the size of the salmon. Ignite and when coals are hot, place fish on grill 5 to 6 inches directly above coals; brush fish with lemon butter. Set pan of butter and a pan with biscuits on a cool area of barbecue. Cover all with a hood or drape with foil. Cook fish about 15 minutes or just until it changes from a bright pink to a paler hue and flakes easily when prodded with a fork in thickest portion. During cooking, brush 3 or 4 times with lemon butter. Move fish from direct heat to cooler area of barbecue and sprinkle with salt and pepper.

Let guests serve themselves by splitting a biscuit, spooning on a little lemon butter, pulling off a piece of fish with a fork, and putting it into the biscuit with a watercress sprig. Makes about 5 dozen appetizers.

CRISP-BAKED ARTICHOKE APPETIZERS

(Pictured on page 4)

Slice fresh, raw artichokes lengthwise to create these unusually shaped appetizers.

    8 small artichokes
       About 1 cup fine dry bread
         crumbs
    1 egg
    ¼ cup water
    ½ teaspoon salt
    ¼ teaspoon pepper
       About 6 tablespoons butter or
         margarine

Wash artichokes; drain. Cut off top halves and trim stems to 1 inch. Snap off tough outer leaves down to pale green leaves; trim base. Slice artichoke in half lengthwise and remove fuzzy choke. Cut each half into ¼-inch-thick lengthwise slices.

Place bread crumbs in a shallow bowl. In another shallow bowl, beat together egg, water, salt, and pepper. Dip each artichoke slice in egg mixture, then in crumbs, coating both sides thoroughly.

Divide butter evenly between two 10 by 15-inch shallow-rimmed baking sheets. Place in a 425° oven just until butter melts. Remove from oven; place half of the artichoke slices in each pan; turn gently to coat both sides with melted butter.

Return to oven and bake, uncovered, for about 15 minutes or until crumbs appear golden brown and crisp. Serve warm.

Or let stand at room temperature up to 3 hours; to reheat, bake, uncovered, in a 425° oven for about 8 minutes or until hot throughout. To eat, hold artichoke by leaves and eat breaded heart. Makes about 2½ dozen.

OLIVE-FILLED CHEESE BALLS

The zing of pimento-stuffed green olives inside a coating of cheese makes these appetizers conversation pieces. They are good when made with ripe olives, too.

    1 cup (4 oz.) shredded sharp
         Cheddar cheese
    2 tablespoons butter or margarine,
         softened
    ½ cup all-purpose flour, unsifted
       Dash of cayenne
   25 medium-size pitted ripe or
         stuffed green olives, well
         drained

Beat together cheese and butter until well blended and creamy. Stir in flour and cayenne. Wrap a teaspoonful of dough around each olive, covering completely. Place 1 inch apart on ungreased baking sheet; bake, uncovered, in a 400° oven for 15 minutes. Makes about 25 appetizers.

CHEDDAR FONDUE APPETIZER CUBES

You can pick up these cheese fondue appetizers with your fingers—they don't drip.

    1 long loaf (about 1 lb.) unsliced
         French bread, 1 to 2 days old
    ½ cup (¼ lb.) butter or margarine
    1 large package (8 oz.) cream
         cheese
    2 cups (8 oz.) shredded sharp
         Cheddar cheese
    ¼ teaspoon garlic or onion powder
         (optional)
    2 egg whites, stiffly beaten

Cut untrimmed bread into cubes about ¾ inch square; set aside. Meanwhile, in top of a double boiler, melt butter and cream cheese over gently boiling water. Gradually add shredded cheese, stirring until melted and smooth. Stir in garlic or onion powder if used. Remove from heat and quickly fold in egg whites.

Keeping top of double boiler over hot water, use 2 forks (fondue forks work well) to quickly dip cubes in cheese, coating them evenly. Tap fork lightly, then place cubes 1 inch apart on wax paper or greased baking sheets. If cheese becomes too thick to coat last cubes, place double boiler over heat just to warm cheese. Let coated cubes stand, uncovered, until dry to the touch (about 2½

hours). If desired, freeze until firm, then package airtight.

To serve, place desired number of cubes (if frozen, don't thaw) on an ungreased baking sheet. Bake, uncovered, in a 350° oven for about 6 to 8 minutes (10 to 12 minutes if frozen) or until hot throughout. Makes about 8 dozen.

HASTY HOTS

(Pictured on page 4)

It takes just a few minutes to put these ever-popular appetizers together.

    4 green onions, finely minced
    ½ cup grated Parmesan cheese
       About 6 tablespoons mayonnaise
       About 2 dozen slices cocktail-
         size rye bread or sliced French
         bread rolls

Stir together onions, cheese, and mayonnaise until well blended, adding more mayonnaise, if necessary, to make firm spreading consistency. Toast one side of bread. Spread cheese mixture on untoasted side and broil about 6 inches below broiler unit until bubbly and lightly browned (about 3 minutes). Makes about 2 dozen appetizers.

PARMESAN POCKET BREAD APPETIZERS

The utter simplicity of this appetizer makes it a favorite for everyone, especially the hostess.

    1 package (12 oz. or 6 slices) Arab
         (pocket) bread
       About ¾ pound butter or mar-
         garine, softened
       About 1½ cups grated Parmesan
         cheese

Cut bread slices in half, then split each half. Spread each bread half with about 1 tablespoon of the butter, sprinkle with about 1 tablespoon of the cheese, and cut into 4 wedges. Put wedges on a baking sheet and bake in a 350° oven for 10 to 15 minutes or until golden brown. Makes 8 dozen.

TOSTADAS DE HARINA

In Mexico and the Southwest, giant-size tortillas are used to make *tostadas de harina* (tortillas with broiled cheese). But regular-size flour tortillas (7 inches in diameter) will work equally well for this recipe and its meaty variations.

- 6 flour tortillas
- 2 cups (about 8 oz.) shredded mild Cheddar cheese
- 2 tablespoons chopped, seeded, canned California green chiles

Evenly sprinkle tortillas with cheese, leaving about a ½-inch margin around edges. Top with chiles. Place on ungreased baking sheets and bake, uncovered, in a 425° oven for 8 to 10 minutes or until edges are crisp and browned. Cut each tortilla into 6 wedges; serve hot. Makes 36 wedges.

Chorizo Tostadas de Harina. Omit green chiles. Remove casings from 2 chorizos; crumble meat and cook over medium heat until lightly browned. Drain meat, discarding fat. Evenly sprinkle cooked chorizo meat over cheese-topped tortillas as in Tostadas de Harina. Bake and cut into wedges.

Carne Seca Tostadas de Harina. Omit green chiles. Crumble ½ can (12-oz. size) corned beef; cook meat over low heat until crisp, stirring occasionally. Evenly sprinkle corned beef over cheese-topped tortillas as in Tostadas de Harina. Bake and cut into wedges.

QUESO AL HORNO

This is a good appetizer to serve at an informal party—you prepare it on the barbecue and guests serve themselves.

Grill the cheese over very slow coals—if the fire is too hot, the cheese will burn on the bottom and boil over. When the cheese has completely melted, invite guests to spread some on a tortilla wedge and top it with a little hot sauce.

- 1 to 1¼ pounds jack cheese
- 3 medium-size tomatoes
- ¼ cup (or to taste) diced canned California green chiles
- 3 tablespoons minced onion
- ½ teaspoon salt
- 2 minced jalapeño chiles (or other hot chiles)
- 1 dozen corn or flour tortillas

Slice cheese into ¼-inch-thick slices and place a single layer in an 8-inch heatproof dish or in a cake or pie pan. Cover and set aside.

To make hot sauce, peel and finely chop tomatoes; mix tomatoes with green chiles, onion, salt, and jalapeño chiles.

Stack tortillas and cut into quarters; wrap in foil. Place in a 350° oven until wedges are soft and warm (about 10 minutes). Keep warm until ready to serve.

Uncover cheese and place over very slow coals (or on a rack set several inches over low-glowing coals) to melt. When cheese is melted, remove from fire or grill. (Return to heat occasionally to keep warm and melted.) To serve, scoop softened cheese onto tortilla wedges; top with a small spoonful of hot sauce. Makes about 48 appetizers.

HAM AND PAPAYA PUPUS

The Hawaiians call their appetizers *pupus*. The term is applied to anything from salted nuts or potato chips to much more elaborate dishes. Here is a simple meat and fruit combination that will delight Island or Mainland cooks.

- ½-pound chunk of cooked ham
- 1 large firm-ripe papaya
  Seasoned butter sauce (recipe follows)

Cut ham into ¾-inch cubes. Peel papaya, cut in half, remove seeds, and cut into ¾-inch cubes. To assemble, thread a papaya cube, then a ham cube onto a wooden pick. (At this point you may cover and refrigerate until next day.)

Dunk pupus in seasoned butter sauce and grill over charcoal 6 to 8 minutes, turning once. Or brush generously with seasoned butter and broil 3 to 4 inches below broiler unit until lightly browned (6 to 8 minutes), turning and basting once. Makes about 3 dozen pupus.

Seasoned Butter Sauce. Combine 3 tablespoons melted butter, 2 tablespoons lemon juice, 2 teaspoons sugar, and ½ teaspoon ground cinnamon.

HEARTY APPETIZER MEATBALLS

(Glazed sausage balls pictured on page 32)

Serving bite-size meatballs from a chafing dish leaves you free to enjoy your party while guests help themselves.

Select one of the three kinds —meatballs with tangy horse-radish sauce, chutney-glazed sausage balls, or lamb meatballs. For a large party, you might set up several chafing dishes and offer a variety of meatballs as appetizers. Provide wooden picks for guests to spear meatballs.

The meatballs can be made ahead and stored as long as 24 hours in the refrigerator or tucked away in the freezer for longer storage.

Lamb Meatballs

- 2 pounds lean ground lamb
- 2 teaspoons *each* ground cumin and salt
- 2 teaspoons chopped fresh mint or 1 teaspoon dried mint
- ¼ cup finely minced green onion
- ¼ teaspoon pepper
- ¼ cup fine dry bread crumbs
- 2 eggs, lightly beaten
- 1 cup sour cream
- 1 teaspoon caraway seed

Stir together lamb, cumin, salt, mint, onion, pepper, bread crumbs, and eggs until well blended. Shape into 1-inch balls. (At this point you may cover and refrigerate until next day, or freeze.)

Place meatballs (thaw if frozen) on rimmed baking sheets and bake, uncovered, in a 425° oven for 15 minutes or until well browned. Reserve meat juices.

Mix together sour cream and caraway seed; transfer to a bowl. Serve meatballs and juices in a chafing dish with sour cream dip alongside. Makes about 5 dozen meatballs.

Glazed Sausage Balls

- ⅓ **pound bulk pork sausage**
- ¾ **pound ground pork or ground beef**
- ½ **teaspoon** *each* **salt, dry mustard, and coriander seed (crushed)**
- ¼ **teaspoon ground allspice**
- 1 **egg, lightly beaten**
- ¼ **cup** *each* **fine dry bread crumbs and thinly sliced green onion**
- ½ **cup** *each* **apple jelly and Major Grey's chutney (finely chopped)**
- 1 **teaspoon lemon juice**

In a bowl, stir together sausage, ground pork, salt, mustard, coriander, allspice, egg, bread crumbs, and onion until well blended. Shape into 1-inch balls. (At this point you may refrigerate until next day, or freeze.)

Place meatballs (thaw if frozen) on rimmed baking sheets and bake, uncovered, in a 500° oven for about 8 minutes or until well browned; drain.

Meanwhile, in a large frying pan over low heat, stir together apple jelly, chutney, and lemon juice; cook, stirring, until jelly is melted. Add meatballs; then cover and simmer for about 8 to 10 minutes or until glazed; transfer to a chafing dish. Makes about 5 dozen meatballs.

Korean Meatballs

- 1 **pound lean ground beef**
- 1 **egg, lightly beaten**
- ¼ **cup** *each* **fine dry bread crumbs and thinly sliced green onion**
- 1 **tablespoon soy sauce**
- ½ **teaspoon** *each* **salt and sugar**
  Horseradish sauce (recipe follows)

In a bowl, stir together ground beef, egg, bread crumbs, onion,

soy, salt, and sugar until well blended. Shape into 1-inch balls. (At this point you may cover and refrigerate until next day, or freeze.)

Place meatballs (thaw if frozen) on rimmed baking sheets and bake, uncovered, in a 500° oven for 4 to 5 minutes or until lightly browned; reserve meat juices. Serve meatballs and reserved juices in a chafing dish with tangy horseradish sauce alongside for dipping. Makes about 5 dozen meatballs.

Horseradish Sauce. In a small bowl, stir together until well blended 2 to 4 tablespoons prepared horseradish, ½ cup thinly sliced green onion, 4 teaspoons dry mustard, ¼ teaspoon salt, and 1 cup unflavored yogurt (or substitute 1 cup sour cream and 1 tablespoon lemon juice). Transfer to bowl deep enough for dipping meatballs.

MARINATED WATER CHESTNUT APPETIZERS

This favorite hors d'oeuvre is a combination of crisp bacon, salty soy sauce, and crunchy water chestnuts.

- 1 **can (5 oz.) water chestnuts, drained**
- ¼ **cup soy sauce**
- 4 **strips bacon**
- ¼ **cup sugar**

Marinate water chestnuts in soy for 30 minutes. Meanwhile cut each bacon strip into fourths by cutting lengthwise, then cross-

wise. Roll each chestnut in sugar, wrap with bacon, and secure with a wooden pick. Place on a rack in a shallow baking pan or on a broiler pan. Bake, uncovered, in a 400° oven for about 20 minutes or until bacon is crisp. Drain on paper towels. Serve warm.

Or cover and refrigerate until next day. To reheat, place on rimmed baking sheets and bake, uncovered, in a 350° oven for about 5 minutes or until crisp and hot throughout. Makes 16 appetizers.

SPICY COCKTAIL WIENERS AND SAUSAGE BALLS

(Wieners pictured on page 5)

Sausage balls or frankfurter chunks are right at home in this pungent sweet and sour sauce.

- 1 **jar (6 oz.) prepared mustard**
- 1 **jar (10 oz.) red currant jelly**
  Sausage balls (recipe follows) or 1 pound frankfurters, cut in 1-inch pieces

Mix together mustard and jelly in a 2-quart pan. Cook over low heat, stirring, until jelly melts. Add either sausage balls or frankfurters and cook, stirring, until meat is heated throughout. Transfer to a chafing dish and keep hot. Offer wooden picks to spear meat. Makes about 3 dozen.

Sausage Balls. Shape 1 pound bulk pork sausage into 1-inch balls. Place on a rimmed baking sheet and bake, uncovered, in a 500° oven for 7 minutes or until well browned. Drain off fat.

SMOKED SALMON FROM THE BARBECUE

(Pictured on page 4)

You can make smoked salmon right at home in your covered barbecue.

> **A 7-pound whole salmon**
> **Salt brine (recipe follows)**
> **Syrup baste (recipe follows)**
> **Fresh or packaged cream cheese**
> **Dark bread or mini-bagels (page 36)**
> **Equipment you'll need: covered barbecue, cheesecloth, small barbecue or old metal pan for igniting extra coals, hickory chips, charcoal briquets, accurate oven thermometer**

Have your fishmonger clean fish, cut off head and tail, and cut fish lengthwise into 2 boneless fillets. Use tweezers to pull out any small remaining bones.

Arrange fillets in a shallow pan; pour over salt brine. Cover and let stand at room temperature 2 to 3 hours or refrigerate as long as 6 hours. Drain fish, rinse in cold water, then pat dry.

Place fillets, skin side down, on several thicknesses of paper towels and let set at room temperature for 30 minutes. Arrange fillets skin side down on a double thickness of cheesecloth, and cut cheesecloth to outline of fish.

Mound 12 charcoal briquets in center of barbecue on lower rack; ignite. Place about 1 cup hickory chips in enough water to cover, and let stand 20 minutes or as long as manufacturer directs.

When coals are completely covered with gray, push 6 of them to one side of the barbecue, 6 to the opposite side (use charcoal racks if you have them to hold coals in place). Drain hickory chips thoroughly; sprinkle about ½ cup over each half of the hot coals.

Grease top grill with oil and set in place. Position salmon fillets, side by side, cheesecloth side down, in center of grill (no part of the fish should be directly over coals); lightly brush fillets with part of syrup baste. Position oven thermometer in center of grill (on top of fillets if necessary); it is very important to maintain 160° to 170° temperature inside the barbecue. Make sure vents of barbecue are open; put cover in place.

Meanwhile, in a separate small barbecue or an old metal pan, ignite 12 more charcoal briquets. Soak another 1 cup hickory chips in enough water to cover. When salmon has smoke-cooked 30 minutes, check thermometer to make sure it reads 160° to 170°. Add about 6 more hot coals to each side of barbecue (more than 6 if temperature has fallen below 160°, fewer than 6 if it has gone above 170°) and sprinkle each half with ½ cup soaked and drained hickory chips. Dab any white juices that have oozed from fish with a paper towel so tops of fillets remain dry and shiny; lightly brush with syrup baste. Cover and continue cooking.

Continue this process of adding hot coals and soaked and drained hickory chips to each side of the barbecue every 30 minutes or as needed to maintain the 160° to 170° temperature inside. Each time you add coals, dab fish with a paper towel to keep top dry; then brush with basting sauce. Continue smoke-cooking fish 2½ to 3 hours or just until fish flakes when prodded with a fork in thickest part.

Gently slide fillets onto flat cooky sheets and let cool slightly at room temperature; then cover and refrigerate as long as 2 weeks. For longer storage, wrap fish securely in a double thickness of foil and freeze.

To serve, transfer cold (defrosted if frozen) fillets to a large serving board; accompany with bread or bagels and fresh cream cheese. Makes about 50 appetizer servings or about 5 pounds smoked salmon.

Salt Brine. In 2 quarts of water, dissolve 1 cup salt and 1½ cups sugar; add 3 tablespoons coarse ground pepper and 3 bay leaves.

Syrup Baste. Stir together 4 tablespoons maple-flavored syrup, 2 tablespoons soy sauce, ¼ teaspoon *each* ground ginger and pepper, and 1 clove garlic, minced or pressed.

RED WINE SIMMERED BEEF CUBES

(Pictured on page 69)

Reminiscent of Boeuf Bourguignon, these hearty beef cubes and onions make a rich, high-protein hors d'oeuvre.

- 3 tablespoons butter or margarine
- About 3½ pounds boneless beef chuck, well trimmed and cut into 1-inch cubes
- 3 tablespoons finely minced shallots or green onion (white part only)
- 1 clove garlic, minced or pressed
- ½ teaspoon *each* salt and thyme leaves
- ¼ teaspoon pepper
- 2 cups dry red wine (such as Burgundy or Gamay)
- About 14 small boiling onions, peeled
- 1 tablespoon cornstarch blended with 1 tablespoon water
- Sliced French bread

In a Dutch oven over medium-high heat, melt half the butter; add half the beef cubes. Cook, turning frequently, until well browned on all sides. Set aside and repeat with remaining butter and beef cubes.

Return all beef cubes to pan; add shallots and garlic and cook, stirring, 1 minute. Add salt, thyme, pepper, and red wine; bring to a boil over high heat. Reduce heat to low, cover, and simmer 45 minutes. Add onions; cover and continue cooking an additional 20 minutes or until beef cubes and onions are fork tender.

Stir cornstarch mixture into beef cubes and sauce; cook, stirring, over high heat until mixture boils and thickens. Transfer to a chafing dish and keep warm. Or cover and chill as long as 2 days; freeze for longer storage. To reheat (thaw if frozen), place in a frying pan over medium heat and simmer until hot throughout.

Serve hot with French bread slices, letting guests make small open-faced sandwiches. Makes about 5 cups.

KOREAN BEEF APPETIZERS

(Pictured on page 73)

This appetizer takes only 2 minutes to cook. Use a very closely spaced grill or a cake rack over the barbecue coals so the meat strips won't fall through; or skewer the meat as shown on page 73.

- 2 tablespoons sesame oil or salad oil
- ¼ cup soy sauce
- 1 teaspoon garlic powder
- 1½ teaspoons vinegar
- Dash of pepper
- 1½ teaspoons toasted sesame seed
- ⅛ to ¼ teaspoon cayenne
- 1 green onion, sliced (including top)
- 1 pound beef chuck, 1½ to 2 inches thick

In a bowl, stir together sesame oil, soy, garlic powder, vinegar, pepper, sesame seed, cayenne, and onion. Cut meat across grain into very thin, 3-inch-long slices. Add to sauce mixture and toss until thoroughly coated. Cover and refrigerate for at least 4 hours or until next day.

To cook, place meat strips (or skewer and place) on a greased grill or rack set 6 inches above a bed of low-glowing coals, or on a gas or electric grill preheated to highest setting. Cook for 1 minute on each side or until brown.

Transfer to a serving platter and provide bamboo skewers or wooden picks for spearing meat. Makes about 2 dozen appetizers.

TAMALE TEMPTERS

Preparing this appetizer is quick and easy—you need only two ingredients.

- 1 can (15 oz.) Mexican-style canned tamales
- 12 strips (about ½ lb.) bacon, cut in half

Remove any husks from tamales and cut into 1-inch lengths; wrap each piece in a strip of bacon and fasten with a wooden pick. Place on a rack on a rimmed baking sheet and broil about 10 minutes, turning once; or bake in a 500° oven for 10 minutes or until bacon is crisp. Makes 2 dozen.

GARLIC PRAWN APPETIZER

You marinate this prawn dish ahead of time, then pop it in the oven when your guests arrive.

- ½ cup olive oil
- 1 clove garlic, minced or pressed
- ¼ teaspoon salt
- 1 pound medium-size (30 to 32 count) prawns, shelled and deveined
- 1 tablespoon finely minced parsley

Stir together oil, garlic, and salt in a shallow baking dish. Add prawns, toss to coat with marinade, and sprinkle parsley over top. Cover and refrigerate at least 4 hours or until next day. Bake casserole, uncovered, in a 375° oven for about 10 minutes or until prawns turn pink. Serve hot, with wooden picks. Makes about 30 appetizers.

ALMOND PRAWNS

Garlic and butter flavor these sautéed prawns; almonds add a crunchy texture; lemon juice piques the flavor.

- ½ cup (¼ lb.) butter or margarine
- 3 cloves garlic, minced or pressed
- ½ cup sliced almonds
- 2 pounds medium-size (about 60–64 count) prawns, shelled and deveined
- ½ cup chopped parsley
- Lemon wedges

Melt butter in a wide frying pan over medium heat. Add garlic and almonds; cook, stirring, until almonds are lightly toasted. Add prawns; keep turning until meat is opaque white throughout (about 5 minutes—cut one to test). Stir in parsley. Transfer to a chafing dish or to a serving dish set on a warming tray. Accompany with lemon wedges. Provide wooden picks to spear prawns. Makes about 5 dozen appetizers.

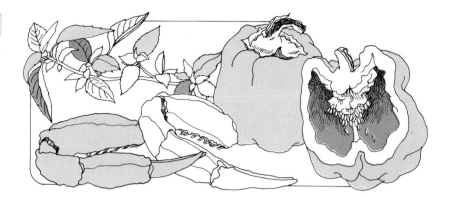

BARBECUED PRAWNS

A sweet and sour sauce flavors these appetizer prawns, which can be either broiled or barbecued.

- 1 can (8 oz.) tomato sauce
- ½ cup molasses
- 1 teaspoon dry mustard
  Salt and pepper to taste
  Few drops liquid hot pepper seasoning
- ¼ cup salad oil
- ⅛ teaspoon thyme leaves
- 2 pounds medium-size (about 60–64 count) prawns, shelled and deveined

Stir together tomato sauce, molasses, mustard, salt, pepper, hot pepper seasoning, salad oil, and thyme until well blended. Add prawns, turning to coat. Cover and refrigerate 4 hours or until next day.

To cook, lift prawns from marinade, thread on skewers, and place on a greased grill 6 inches away from low-glowing coals or on a rimmed baking sheet 6 inches below broiler unit. Grill or broil, basting frequently and turning once, until prawns turn pink (about 4 minutes on each side). Makes about 5 dozen appetizers.

BACON-WRAPPED PRAWNS

Freshly cooked prawns, seasoned and wrapped in bacon, make delicious party tidbits. You can prepare these ahead of time, then refrigerate them until time to broil and serve.

- 1 pound medium-size (30–32 count) prawns
  Boiling water
  About ½ pound sliced bacon
- 1 clove garlic, minced or pressed
- ½ cup tomato-based chile sauce

Cook prawns in enough boiling water to cover until they turn pink (about 5 minutes). Drain and cool; shell and devein. Cook bacon strips in a frying pan over medium heat just until limp; drain and cut each slice in half

crosswise. Stir together garlic and chile sauce until well blended. Dip each prawn into sauce to coat, wrap in half strip of bacon, and secure with a wooden pick. (At this point you may cover and refrigerate until next day.)

To cook, place appetizers on a broiler pan or on a rack set over a shallow baking pan. Broil 6 inches below a preheated broiler unit, turning once, until bacon is crisp (about 5 minutes). Serve hot. Makes about 2½ dozen appetizers.

SPICY-MINT GRILLED PRAWNS

These prawn appetizers—marinated in a minty mixture—can be either grilled or broiled.

- 1 teaspoon ground chile powder
- 1 tablespoon vinegar
- ¼ teaspoon pepper
- 1 clove garlic, minced or pressed
- 1 teaspoon *each* salt and dry basil
- 1 tablespoon finely chopped fresh mint *or* 1½ teaspoons dry mint
- ¾ cup salad oil
- 2 pounds medium-size (about 60–64 count) prawns, shelled and deveined

In a bowl, stir together chile powder, vinegar, pepper, garlic, salt, basil, mint, and oil until well blended. Add prawns, turning to coat. Cover and refrigerate for at least 4 hours or until next day.

To cook, remove prawns from marinade and thread on skewers (reserve marinade). Place prawns on a greased grill set 6 inches above a bed of low-glowing coals (or on a broiler pan or a rack over

a shallow baking pan set 6 inches below a preheated broiler unit). Grill or broil, basting frequently with reserved marinade and turning once, until prawns turn pink (about 4 minutes on each side). Makes about 5 dozen appetizers.

LEMON ALMOND SCALLOPS

This poached scallop idea, Hawaiian in origin, features scallops speared with a wooden pick, swished in a butter mixture, and dipped in almonds.

- 1 pound scallops, rinsed and drained
- ⅓ cup blanched almonds
  Water
- 3 tablespoons melted butter or margarine
- 2 tablespoons lemon juice

Tear scallops into bite-size pieces; drain on paper towels and refrigerate until cooking time. Place almonds on a rimmed baking sheet and bake in a 350° oven for 7 minutes or until lightly toasted. Cool; then chop finely and set aside.

Poach scallop pieces in enough simmering water to cover until they lose their transparency and turn opaque and milky white (about 2 to 3 minutes—break one in half to test). Drain well. Place on a serving plate set on a warming tray. Stir together butter and lemon juice until blended.

To serve, let guests spear a scallop piece with a wooden pick, swish in lemon-butter mixture, then dip in toasted almonds. Makes about 4 dozen appetizers.

CLAMS OR OYSTERS CASINO

Simplicity is the key to this dramatic appetizer. Plan to prepare it when you want a real show-stopper hors d'oeuvre.

    Rock salt
12 **whole clams or oysters**
    Salt
¼ **cup** *each* **chopped green and red pepper**
 3 **strips bacon, quartered**
    Lemon wedges

Half fill a shallow 3-quart baking dish with rock salt. Heat salt-filled dish in a 400° oven for 20 minutes. Open clams or oysters (or have it done at the market) and discard top shells. Leave meat and juices in bottom shells and place them open-side-up on salt so they are level.

Combine green and red pepper. Sprinkle each mollusk with about 1 teaspoon of the pepper mixture and top with a piece of bacon. Return dish to a 400° oven and bake for about 15 minutes or until bacon is crisp. (Do not overcook.) Serve with wedges of lemon. Provide forks or wooden picks. Makes 1 dozen appetizers.

CRAB AND CHEESE ROUNDS

Cocktail-size rye bread topped with a cheese and crab mixture makes an easy-to-assemble hot appetizer.

    About 3 dozen slices of cocktail-size rye bread
    About 5 tablespoons butter or margarine
 2 **cups (about 1 lb.) cooked or canned crab**
½ **cup sour cream**
 3 **teaspoons lemon juice**
½ **teaspoon Worcestershire**
    Dash liquid hot pepper seasoning
1½ **cups (about 6 oz.) shredded Swiss cheese**
    Paprika

Toast bread on one side until lightly brown; lightly spread with some of the butter. Combine crab, sour cream, lemon juice, Worcestershire, hot pepper seasoning, and 1 cup of the cheese. Spread about 1 tablespoon of crab-cheese mixture on each slice of bread; evenly sprinkle remaining ½ cup cheese on top of crab mixture; then sprinkle lightly with paprika. Place on a baking sheet and bake, uncovered, in a 400° oven for about 8 minutes or until hot and bubbly. Serve hot. Makes about 3 dozen appetizers.

DEEP-FRIED CRAB PUFFS

Biscuit mix and Parmesan cheese form the basis for these highly seasoned, deep-fried crab puffs. Serve them warm right after frying or freeze them until the day of your party. Present with a bowl of creamy mustard sauce for dipping.

1½ **cups biscuit mix (baking mix)**
⅓ **cup grated Parmesan cheese**
¼ **cup finely chopped green onion**
 1 **cup (about 8 oz.) cooked or canned crab**
 1 **egg**
⅓ **cup water**
 1 **teaspoon Worcestershire**
¼ **teaspoon liquid hot pepper seasoning**
    Salad oil
    Mustard dip (recipe follows)

Stir together biscuit mix, cheese, and onion. Shred crab and stir into cheese mixture. Beat together egg, water, Worcestershire, and hot pepper seasoning. Stir into crab mixture just until blended.

In a deep pan, heat about 1½ inches oil to 375° on a deep-fat-frying thermometer. Fry 3 or 4 puffs at a time by dropping teaspoonfuls of batter into hot oil. Cook, turning as necessary, until golden brown on all sides (about 1½ to 2 minutes). Lift out with a slotted spoon; drain on paper towels. Keep in a 200° oven until all are fried. Serve warm.

Or cool, package airtight, and freeze. To reheat (thaw if frozen), place on a baking sheet and bake, uncovered, for about 7 minutes or until hot. Serve with Mustard Dip. Makes about 3 dozen.

Mustard Dip. Stir together ½ cup sour cream, 2 tablespoons Dijon mustard, and 1 teaspoon lemon juice until blended.

PASTRY CRAB PUFFS

(Pictured on page 80)

Chou paste, a simple dough, forms the base for these puffs.

½ **cup water**
⅛ **teaspoon salt**
 2 **tablespoons butter or margarine**
 6 **drops liquid hot pepper seasoning**
½ **cup sifted, all-purpose flour**
 2 **eggs**
 1 **tablespoon finely minced green onion tops or chives**
 1 **cup (about 8 oz.) cooked or canned crab**
    Salad oil
    About 1 cup homemade guacamole (see page 11) or thawed frozen avocado dip

Put water, salt, butter, and hot pepper seasoning in a 2-quart saucepan. Bring mixture to a full rolling boil over high heat; add flour all at once, remove pan from heat, and stir vigorously until mixture forms a ball and leaves sides of pan. Beat in eggs, one at a time, until mixture is smooth and shiny. Add onion and crab; stir until blended. Cool about 15 minutes.

In a deep pan, heat 1½ to 2 inches oil to 370° on a deep-fat-frying thermometer. Drop teaspoonfuls of dough into hot oil and fry, turning occasionally, until golden brown on all sides (about 3 minutes). With a slotted spoon, remove from oil and drain. Keep in a 200° oven until all are fried. Serve warm.

Or cool completely, cover and refrigerate until next day; for longer storage, wrap airtight and freeze. To reheat (thaw if frozen), place on a baking sheet and bake, uncovered, in a 350° oven for about 7 minutes or until hot. Offer wooden picks to spear puffs and guacamole to dip puffs into. Makes about 3 dozen appetizers.

TOFU TUNA PUFFS

Tofu, high-protein soybean curd cake, forms the basis for these puffy appetizers. Tofu is available at oriental food stores and in markets well stocked with oriental products.

> About 1 pound medium-firm
>   tofu
> 1 can (about 6½ oz.) tuna
> 1 egg
> 2 tablespoons finely minced green
>   onion
> 1 tablespoon finely chopped fresh
>   coriander *or* 2 teaspoons dry
>   cilantro leaves
> 1 teaspoon baking powder
> ½ teaspoon salt
> ¼ teaspoon pepper
>   Salad oil
>   Soy sauce

In a colander, drain tofu as much as possible (about ½ hour). Press through a fine wire strainer and into a bowl, or thoroughly mash with a fork. Discard any liquid. Drain and flake tuna and add to tofu, stirring until well blended.

In another bowl beat together egg, onion, coriander, baking powder, salt, and pepper. Add egg mixture to tofu and tuna, stirring until well blended. Form into 1-inch balls and place on paper towels for tofu to drain further.

In a deep pan, heat oil to 375° on a deep-fat-frying thermometer. Lower tofu balls into hot oil and cook until golden brown (about 2 to 3 minutes). Drain on paper towels. Serve hot.

Or cool thoroughly, cover, and refrigerate until next day. To reheat, place puffs on a rimmed baking sheet and bake in a 300° oven for 10 minutes or until hot throughout. Serve with wooden picks and soy sauce for dipping. Makes about 3 dozen puffs.

TUNA BALLS WITH CHEESE DIP

A creamy cheese sauce made from a pasteurized cheese spread accompanies these crisp tuna appetizers.

> 1 can (about 6½ oz.) tuna, well
>   drained
> ½ cup fine dry bread crumbs
> 2 tablespoons *each* minced onion
>   and parsley
> 2 teaspoons prepared mustard
> 3 tablespoons mayonnaise
> ½ teaspoon poultry seasoning
> ¼ teaspoon liquid hot pepper sea-
>   soning
> 1 egg, lightly beaten
> 3 tablespoons melted butter or
>   margarine
> ½ cup crushed corn flakes
>   Hot cheese dip (recipe follows)

Flake tuna with a fork. Stir in crumbs, onion, parsley, mustard, mayonnaise, poultry seasoning, hot pepper seasoning, and egg until well blended.

Shape into balls, using about 2 teaspoons for each. Dip balls in butter and roll in corn flakes to coat thoroughly.

Place 1 inch apart on an ungreased baking sheet and bake, uncovered, in a 450° oven for about 8 to 10 minutes (12 if chilled) or until hot and crisp. Serve hot with cheese dip. Makes about 2 dozen appetizers.

Hot Cheese Dip. In small pan or fondue pot, combine 2 jars (5 oz. *each*) sharp pasteurized process cheese spread and ⅓ cup milk. Cook over low heat, stirring, until cheese is melted and bubbly.

SNAILS ON TOAST

Tiny rectangles of toast serve as edible platters for buttery snails.

> 6 slices firm white bread
>   Herb butter (recipe follows)
> 1 can (at least 24 count)
>   snails, drained
>   About ¼ cup shredded Swiss
>   cheese

Trim crusts from bread; then cut each slice into quarters. Place on a baking sheet and bake in a 350° oven until lightly toasted on both sides (about 12 to 15 minutes total). Spread one side of each piece of toast with herb butter, using about half the butter; top each

with a snail. Dot snails evenly with remaining butter, then sprinkle evenly with cheese. Return to a 350° oven until cheese melts (about 3 minutes). Serve warm. Makes about 2 dozen.

Herb Butter. In a small bowl, stir together until blended 6 tablespoons butter or margarine (softened), ¼ teaspoon dry basil, 1 small clove garlic (minced or pressed), 1 tablespoon minced shallots *or* green onion, and 2 tablespoons minced parsley.

SNAILS WITH HERB BUTTER

(Pictured on opposite page)

Canned snails are sold without shells, but you can purchase reusable natural or ceramic shells as well as canned snails at import or gourmet shops. Provide tiny forks to pull out the snails.

> 1 can (18 count) extra-large
>   snails
> ½ cup (¼ lb.) butter or margarine,
>   softened
> 2 small cloves garlic, minced or
>   pressed
> 2 teaspoons chopped chives or
>   green onion tops
> 1 tablespoon minced parsley
> 18 clean, dry snail shells, real or ar-
>   tificial
> 6 to 8 tablespoons grated Parmesan
>   cheese

Drain snails, rinse, then drain thoroughly on paper towels.

Stir together butter, garlic, chives, and parsley until well blended. Put a small bit of seasoned butter mixture in each shell and then tuck in a snail. Seal in with remaining butter mixture, dividing evenly among snails. Press buttered surface firmly into grated cheese.

Place shells, cheese side up, in snail pans (three 6-snail size, or one 12-snail size plus one 6-snail size) or individual baking pans.

To serve, bake, uncovered, in a 500° oven for 5 minutes or until cheese is lightly browned and butter is bubbly. Serve hot. If desired, serve on sliced French bread or rolls. Makes 18 appetizers.

Snails with Herb Butter make elegant appetizer fare.
Serve with sliced French bread and white wine.
(Recipe on page 48)

CRISPY CHICKEN WING APPETIZERS

When you cut the meatiest sections of chicken wings to resemble tiny drumsticks and then fry them, they make amusing and tempting appetizers.

Once you get the rhythm of trimming the wings, the process goes quickly. It can be done a day ahead.

> About 4½ pounds chicken wings
> Salt and pepper
> Cornstarch
> Salad oil
> Bottled spicy barbecue sauce

Cut off meatiest portion of chicken wings at first joint (reserve center sections and tips to make stock another time).

Holding small end of each large piece, trim around bone with sharp knife to cut meat free. Then cut and scrape with knife to push meat down to large end of bone. Finally, with your fingers, pull portion of meat and skin down over end of bone. (At this point you can cover and refrigerate wings until next day.)

Just before frying, sprinkle wings lightly with salt and pepper, then dust with cornstarch; shake off excess. In a deep pan, heat 1½ inches oil to 350° on a deep-fat-frying thermometer. Cook 4 or 5 wings at a time for 5 to 6 minutes or until golden brown, turning several times. Lift from oil with a slotted spoon and drain on paper towels; keep warm in a 200° oven until all are cooked or as long as 1 hour. Serve warm with a barbecue sauce for dipping. Makes about 2 dozen appetizers.

BAKED CHICKEN LIVERS WITH MUSTARD SAUCE

Crushed cheese-flavored crackers make a crisp coating for these baked chicken livers, dipped in a tangy, mustard-seasoned tartar sauce.

> 1 pound chicken livers
> Cheese-flavored crackers
> ½ teaspoon seasoned salt
> 2 tablespoons melted butter or margarine
> Mustard sauce (recipe follows)

Cut chicken livers in half; rinse and drain on paper towels. Crush enough crackers to make ¾ cup fine crumbs. Mix together crumbs, salt, and butter. Roll livers in crumb mixture to coat evenly, then place on an ungreased rimmed baking sheet without crowding.

Bake, uncovered, in a 425° oven for about 12 minutes or until still slightly pink inside (cut a gash to test). Serve hot with wooden picks. Accompany with mustard sauce. Makes about 20 appetizers.

Mustard Sauce. Stir together until well blended ½ cup prepared tartar sauce, 2 tablespoons Dijon mustard, ¼ cup milk, and 2 tablespoons chopped chives or chopped green onion tops. Cover and chill until next day, if desired.

EASY RUMAKI

A departure from the traditional rumaki, this recipe uses a simplified marinade—soy sauce and Vermouth. In assembling the morsels, sandwich the chicken liver pieces between water chestnut halves. The rumaki can be either broiled or grilled.

> ½ pound chicken livers
> ½ cup dry Vermouth
> 2 cans (4 to 5 oz. *each*) water chestnuts (about 16), drained
> 8 strips bacon
> ⅓ cup soy sauce

Cut chicken livers into 16 bite-size pieces; rinse and drain on paper towels. Heat 2 tablespoons of the Vermouth in a frying pan over medium heat; add liver pieces and cook, stirring, until lightly browned but still pink inside (cut a gash to test); drain. Cut 16 water chestnuts in half (reserve any remaining for other uses). Cut bacon strips in half crosswise.

Sandwich a piece of chicken liver between 2 water chestnut halves; wrap with bacon and fasten with a wooden pick. Combine soy and remaining Vermouth. Pour over skewered livers in a shallow bowl and let stand at least 1 hour, basting occasionally; or cover and refrigerate as long as 8 hours.

Remove rumaki from marinade and place on a grill set 6 inches above a bed of low-glowing coals or on a rack in a shallow pan set 6 inches below preheated broiler unit. Grill or broil until bacon is crisp (about 6 minutes). Makes 16 appetizers.

JAPANESE RUMAKI

You can assemble these Japanese rumaki ahead, then refrigerate them until time to broil. Serve them as is or with a hot mustard for dipping.

> ¾ pound chicken livers
> ½ pound sliced bacon
> 1 can (6½ oz.) whole water chestnuts, drained
> ½ cup soy sauce
> 1 small clove garlic, minced or pressed
> 1 small dried hot chile pepper, crushed
> 6 thin slices peeled fresh ginger
> Hot Chinese-style or Dijon mustard (optional)

Cut chicken livers in half; rinse and drain on paper towels. Cut each bacon strip in half crosswise. Fold each piece of liver around a water chestnut, wrap with bacon, and fasten with a wooden pick.

Stir together soy, garlic, chile pepper, and ginger. Add chicken liver bundles; cover and refrigerate, turning occasionally, for at least 3 hours or until next day.

Place rumaki on a broiler pan or on a rack in a shallow baking pan and broil 6 inches below a preheated broiler unit, turning once, until bacon is crisp (about 7 minutes). Serve hot, with mustard for dipping, if desired. Makes about 18 appetizers.

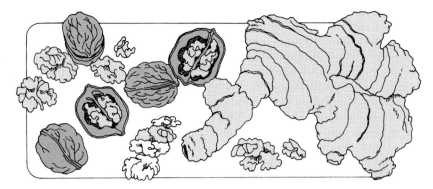

CHICKEN WINGS TERIYAKI

(Pictured on page 53)

To make these appetizers, you separate chicken wings into two meaty sections, marinate and cook them in a teriyaki sauce, and then grill them over coals.

> 3 pounds chicken wings
> ½ cup soy sauce
> ¼ cup *each* Vermouth and un-sweetened pineapple juice
> 2 cloves garlic, minced or pressed
> 1 tablespoon firmly packed brown sugar
> ¼ teaspoon ground ginger
> 1 tablespoon *each* cornstarch and water

Remove tips from chicken wings (reserve to make stock another time); cut each wing in half at first joint. (Or skewer wings as shown on page 53. Straighten wings by forcing joints until connective tissue snaps. Thread skewers through meat of chicken along bone from wide end of wing to tip.)

In a deep bowl or baking pan, stir together soy, Vermouth, pineapple juice, garlic, brown sugar, and ginger until blended. Add wings and turn them to coat evenly. Cover and refrigerate at least 12 hours or until next day, turning several times.

To bake, place wings in a single layer in a 9 by 13-inch baking pan; pour marinade over. Bake, uncovered, in a 325° oven for 25 minutes or until meat is tender when pierced with a fork; drain off and reserve marinade.

In a small pan, stir together cornstarch and water; gradually stir in reserved marinade. Cook, stirring, until sauce boils, thickens, and clears. Brush sauce on wings. (At this point you may cover and refrigerate up to 6 hours.)

To brown wings, place them on a grill about 6 inches above a bed of low-glowing coals, or place on a gas or electric grill pre-heated to highest setting. Cook, turning, until browned and crispy (about 2 minutes on each side). Makes about 2 dozen appetizers.

INDONESIAN CHICKEN

(Pictured on page 73)

An adaptation of a classic Indonesian entrée, this appetizer features chicken coated with a nut mixture, broiled or grilled, and served with a nut-yogurt sauce.

> 2 whole (about ¾ lb. *each*) chicken breasts, boned
> 2 cups chopped walnuts
> ⅔ cup lime juice
> 2 tablespoons regular-strength chicken broth
> 2 green onions, cut into pieces
> 2 small cloves garlic, minced or pressed
> ½ teaspoon salt
> 1 cup yogurt or sour cream

Cut chicken into bite-size pieces; set aside. Put walnuts, lime juice, broth, onion, garlic, and salt in a blender and whirl until walnuts are quite fine. Stir ½ cup of nut mixture into yogurt to serve as a dip with chicken; cover and chill.

Gently coat pieces of chicken with remaining nut mixture. Then thread coated chicken pieces onto skewers. (At this point, you may cover and chill until next day.)

To cook, place chicken skewers on a greased grill set 6 inches above a bed of low-glowing coals or on a shallow baking pan 6 inches below a preheated broiler unit. Grill or broil chicken, turning once, until chicken is opaque (about 6 minutes altogether).

Transfer to a serving platter and serve with wooden picks and yogurt sauce for dipping. Makes about 30 appetizers.

FALAFIL

For those with an adventuresome palate, here is an interesting appetizer common to the southeastern shores of the Mediterranean.

Falafil are fried morsels made from a highly seasoned legume flour that's laced with crunchy sesame seed. The flour is available as a dry mix in markets that specialize in foods of the Near East. You simply add water, shape small balls of the falafil, and fry in oil.

> 1 cup dry falafil mix
> ½ cup water
> Salad oil
> Unflavored yogurt or yogurt sauce (recipe follows)

Stir together falafil mix and water until water is well absorbed; then shape into ¾-inch balls. In a small deep pan, heat 1 inch of salad oil to 350° on a deep-fat-frying thermometer.

Immerse falafil balls gently in oil; do not crowd pan. Cook about 2½ minutes or until browned; drain on paper towels. Serve hot.

Or cover with clear plastic film and refrigerate until next day; freeze for longer storage. To reheat, place falafil (refrigerated or thawed frozen) on a rimmed baking sheet and bake, uncovered, in a 350° oven for 5 minutes or until hot throughout. Serve plain or with Yogurt Sauce. Makes about 40 appetizers.

Yogurt Sauce. Combine ½ cup unflavored yogurt and 1½ tablespoons *each* minced green onion and peeled cucumber.

LUMPIA APPETIZERS

(Pictured on page 73)

Filipino dishes often have a Chinese counterpart, and that's true of *lumpia*, a Filipino appetizer similar to Chinese won ton. The easiest way to make lumpia is with won ton skins, available in the produce section of markets stocked with oriental products.

Lumpia filling (recipe follows)
Dipping sauce (recipe follows)
1 **package (1 lb.) won ton skins**
Salad oil

Prepare filling and dipping sauce as directed. Drain juices from filling, retaining ¼ cup juices. Then stir ¼ cup of the dipping sauce into the filling.

Mound about 1 teaspoon filling in lower corner of won ton skin (cover remaining won ton skins with a damp cloth to keep supple). Fold corner over filling and roll, tucking in ends. (At this point you may place on a baking sheet, cover with clear plastic film, and refrigerate as long as 8 hours; freeze for longer storage.)

To fry, heat ¼ inch oil in a wide frying pan over medium heat. Set in lumpia (freshly made, refrigerated, or thawed frozen), seam sides down, and fry, turning to brown evenly (1 to 2 minutes). Drain on paper towels. Keep warm in a 200° oven until all are cooked.

Meanwhile, stir the reserved ¼ cup juices from filling into dipping sauce and reheat to boiling over high heat. Serve hot or warm with warm lumpia.

Lumpia Filling. Crumble ¾ pound ground fresh pork into a frying pan; add 1 medium-size onion (chopped) and 3 cloves garlic (minced or pressed) and cook, stirring, over medium heat until meat is brown and crumbly and onion is limp. Stir in 6 ounces shelled, deveined, chopped raw prawns; cook, stirring, for 2 minutes. Stir in ¾ cup coarsely chopped bean sprouts and cook 2 minutes more. Stir in 1½ table-spoons soy sauce; remove from heat. Cover and refrigerate until next day, if you wish.

Dipping Sauce. Stir together 2 tablespoons cornstarch and ¼ cup packed brown sugar. Stir in ½ cup *each* cold water and pineapple (or orange) juice and ¼ cup *each* vinegar and soy sauce until blended. Heat 1 tablespoon salad oil in a frying pan over medium heat, add 2 cloves garlic (minced or pressed), and cook, stirring, until lightly browned. Add sauce mixture to pan and cook, stirring, until sauce boils and thickens. Cover and refrigerate until next day, if you wish.

TOFU TERIYAKI APPETIZERS

(Pictured on page 73)

Teriyaki sauce glazes raw-fried tofu in this simple, flavorful appetizer.

Raw-fried tofu is highly compressed soybean curd that has been fried in hot oil. You'll find it in oriental grocery stores or in markets that are well stocked with oriental products.

About ¼ cup sesame seed
2 **tablespoons dry Sherry**
2 **teaspoons cornstarch**
⅓ **cup soy sauce**
2 **cloves garlic, minced or pressed**
¼ **cup firmly packed brown sugar**
¼ **teaspoon dry mustard**
1 **teaspoon grated fresh ginger or**
½ **teaspoon ground ginger**
1 **pound raw-fried tofu**

In a small pan over medium heat, stir sesame seed until lightly toasted; remove from pan and set aside. In the pan, stir together Sherry and cornstarch; stir in soy, garlic, brown sugar, dry mustard, and ginger and cook, stirring, over medium heat until mixture boils and thickens; cool. Pour sauce over raw-fried tofu in a shallow pan to coat thoroughly on all sides; cover pan tightly and marinate for about 1 hour.

Before serving, lift tofu from sauce and place on a rack set over a shallow baking pan or on a broiler pan. Broil 3 inches below a preheated broiler unit until sauce bubbles (about 2 minutes on each side); baste occasionally with remaining sauce. Cut tofu into ¾-inch cubes. Sprinkle with sesame seed. Serve warm with wooden picks for spearing. Makes about 4 dozen appetizers.

VEGETABLE MORSELS

This nutrient-rich mixture of vegetables and egg produces appetizers somewhat similar to the popular *falafil* of the Near and Middle East. Though they lack legume flour, they are served in the same way, with yogurt for dipping.

3 **eggs**
2 **teaspoons onion salt or salt**
1 **teaspoon ground cumin**
¼ **teaspoon pepper**
3 **tablespoons *each* sesame seed, wheat germ, and all-purpose flour (unsifted)**
2 **cups shredded carrots**
1 **package (10 oz.) frozen chopped spinach (thawed and extra moisture squeezed out)**
1 **package (10 oz.) frozen green beans (thawed, extra moisture squeezed out, and chopped) *or* 1½ cups chopped cooked green beans**
1 **cup unflavored yogurt**

Stir together eggs, salt, cumin, pepper, sesame seed, wheat germ, flour, carrots, spinach, and beans until well blended.

Shape mixture into 1-inch balls; place 1 inch apart on well-greased rimmed baking pans. Bake, uncovered, in a 450° oven for 10 minutes or until lightly browned. Serve warm.

Or cool, cover, and refrigerate up to 3 days; wrap airtight and freeze for longer storage. To reheat, arrange chilled or thawed morsels in a single layer in a shallow baking pan and place in a 350° oven for 10 minutes or until hot throughout.

Serve with yogurt and wooden picks for dipping. Makes about 5 dozen morsels.

Outdoor barbecue acts as host and server for hearty high-protein appetizers: Italian Sausage and Cheese (page 40), Pop-open Clams (page 40), and skewered Chicken Wings Teriyaki (page 51).

CHINESE WON TON

(Pictured on page 73)

These won ton appetizers call for purchased won ton dough (available in 1-pound packages in the produce section of markets well stocked with oriental products) and a pork or shrimp filling.

> **Pork, shrimp, or chorizo sausage and beef filling (recipes follow)**
> 1 **package (1 lb.) won ton skins**
> 1 **egg, beaten**
> **Salad oil**
> **Sauces for dipping (suggestions accompany each filling recipe)**

Prepare filling of your choice as directed.

Following illustrations below, 1) hold won ton skin in your hand (cover remaining won ton skins with a damp towel to keep them supple). Mound 1 teaspoon filling in corner near palm of hand. Dot that corner with egg. 2) Fold egg-moistened corner over filling, rolling to tuck point under. 3) Turn; moisten both corners at filling ends with egg. 4) Bring these corners together, overlapping slightly. Pinch together firmly to seal. Repeat until all won ton skins are filled.

Place filled won ton side by side on a tray and cover with clear plastic film. (At this point, you may refrigerate as long as 8 hours or package airtight and freeze.)

To fry, heat about 2 inches of oil in a deep pan to 360° on a deep-fat-frying thermometer. Add 4 to 6 won ton (freshly made, refrigerated, or thawed frozen) to oil; fry 1 to 2 minutes or until golden brown, turning to cook evenly. Lift from oil with a slotted spoon and drain on paper towels. Keep warm in a 200° oven until all are cooked; then serve warm.

Or cool completely, package airtight, and freeze. To reheat, place frozen won ton in a single layer on a shallow baking sheet and bake, uncovered, in a 350° oven for about 15 minutes or until crisp and hot throughout. Makes 5 to 7 dozen won ton.

Pork Filling. In a frying pan over medium heat, stir 1 pound lean ground pork until brown and crumbly. Stir in 1 can (5 or 6 oz.) water chestnuts, chopped and drained; 2 green onions, thinly sliced; 2 tablespoons soy sauce; and ¼ teaspoon garlic salt until well blended. Stir together 1 tablespoon dry Sherry and 1 teaspoon cornstarch; stir into pork mixture and cook, stirring, for about 1 minute. Cool filling; then wrap and fry as directed. Serve with hot mustard and catsup (separately) for dipping. Fills 6 to 7 dozen won ton.

Shrimp Filling. Finely chop 1 pound shelled and deveined raw prawns. Stir in 1 can (5 or 6 oz.) water chestnuts, chopped and drained; 2 green onions, thinly sliced; 2 tablespoons soy sauce; and ⅛ teaspoon garlic salt until well blended. Wrap and fry as directed. Serve with chile sauce or tartar sauce for dipping. Fills 5 to 6 dozen won ton.

Chorizo Sausage and Beef Filling. Remove casings from 2 chorizo sausages (or enough to make 6 oz. meat). Crumble sausage in a frying pan, add ½ pound lean ground beef, and cook, stirring, over medium heat until crumbly and brown (about 5 minutes). Stir in 1 green onion, thinly sliced; 2 canned California green chiles, seeded and chopped; and ½ cup shredded jack cheese until well blended. Cook, stirring, until cheese melts. Cool filling; then wrap and fry as directed. Serve with homemade guacamole (page 11) or thawed frozen avocado dip. Fills 5 to 6 dozen won ton.

SPRING ROLLS

Thanks to ready-to-fill wrappers, the Chinese pastry appetizers known as spring roll or egg roll are easy to duplicate at home.

The spring roll wrapper skins—similar to won ton skins, but larger—are available in oriental markets and in the refrigerator or freezer section of many supermarkets.

> **Ham or beef filling (recipes follow)**
> 1 **package (1 lb.) spring roll or egg roll skins**
> 1 **egg, beaten**
> **Salad oil**
> **Sweet and sour sauce (recipe follows) or soy sauce**

Prepare your choice of filling as directed.

To fill each spring roll, place a skin on a flat surface with a corner pointing toward you; mound about 2 rounded tablespoons of cooled filling across skin in a 3½-inch log, about 2 inches above lower corner. Fold this corner over filling to cover, then roll over once to enclose filling. Using a chopstick or your finger, dot left and right corners of triangle with egg; fold corners over filling, pressing firmly to seal. Moisten remaining corner of skin with

How to fold won ton

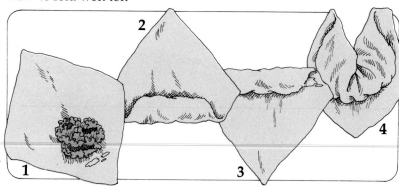

egg, then roll, sealing corner. Cover filled rolls with clear plastic film until ready to fry. Refrigerate until next day, if desired.

To fry rolls, heat 1 inch salad oil in a frying pan to 370° on a deep-fat-frying thermometer. Fry 4 to 6 rolls at a time, turning as needed, until golden brown (about 4 minutes). Drain well on several layers of paper towels; keep in a 200° oven until all are cooked.

To serve, cut rolls into thirds. Serve warm with sweet and sour sauce or soy sauce.

Or cool thoroughly, wrap airtight, and freeze. To reheat, place frozen rolls in a single layer in a shallow rimmed baking pan; bake, uncovered, for about 25 minutes or until hot. Drain thoroughly. Makes about 2 dozen.

Ham Filling. Heat 2 tablespoons salad oil in a large frying pan over medium-high heat. Add 1 clove garlic (minced or pressed), ½ teaspoon grated fresh ginger or ¼ teaspoon ground ginger, 1 large onion (chopped), and 1 cup thinly sliced celery; cook, stirring, for 1 minute. Drain 1 can (6 oz.) bamboo shoots and cut them into matchstick-size slivers. Add 2 cups finely shredded cabbage and 1 pound cooked ham (cut into matchstick-size slivers); cook, stirring, for 2 minutes. Mix together 1 tablespoon cornstarch, ½ teaspoon salt, 2 teaspoons soy, and 1 tablespoon dry Sherry. Stir into vegetable mixture and cook, stirring, for 1 minute longer. Cool. Cover and refrigerate until next day, if desired.

Beef Filling. Heat 1 tablespoon salad oil in a large frying pan. Add 1 pound lean ground beef; stir to break up meat and cook until lightly browned. Add 1 large onion (chopped) and 2 cloves garlic (minced or pressed); cook 1 minute, stirring. Then add 3 cups *each* shredded zucchini and cabbage; cook 2 minutes. Mix together 1 tablespoon *each* cornstarch and soy, 1 teaspoon *each* sugar and salt, and ½ teaspoon pepper; add to meat mixture and cook, stirring constantly, for 1 minute. Cool. Cover and refrigerate until next day, if desired.

Sweet and Sour Sauce. In a small pan, stir together until blended 1½ teaspoons cornstarch, 3 tablespoons *each* sugar and wine vinegar, 1 tablespoon *each* soy and chile sauce, a dash of cayenne, and ½ cup regular-strength chicken broth. Cook, stirring, over high heat until thick and clear.

INDIAN SAMOSAS

Spicy, meat-filled, fried pastries, *samosas* are popular snacks in India. Cooks there use thin circles of dough, but oriental won ton skins (available in the produce section of markets well stocked with oriental products) are a quick and easy alternative to the dough circles.

Samosas can be made ahead, then refrigerated or frozen until time to fry. Or you can do the frying in advance and simply reheat them in the oven before serving.

    1½ pounds lean ground beef
    1 large onion, finely chopped
    3 cloves garlic, minced or pressed
    3 tablespoons ground curry powder
    1½ teaspoons *each* salt and ground ginger
    1 teaspoon sugar
    ¼ teaspoon cayenne
    1 package (10 oz.) frozen peas, thawed
    1 package (1 lb.) won ton skins
    Water
    Salad oil
    Yogurt sauce (recipe follows)

In a large frying pan over medium heat, cook and stir beef until brown and crumbly. Add onion, garlic, curry, salt, ginger, sugar, and cayenne; cook, stirring, until onion is limp. Stir in peas and cook 1 minute. Drain off and discard any fat. Let filling cool.

In one corner of a won ton skin, mound 1 scant tablespoon filling (cover remaining won ton skins with a damp cloth to keep them supple). With your finger, moisten with water that corner and two edges of skin surrounding filling. Bring opposite corner of won ton skin over filling and press edges together, sealing them to form a triangle. Continue until all won ton skins are filled. (At this point you may place filled samosas on a tray, wrap tightly with clear plastic film, and refrigerate as long as 8 hours or freeze for longer storage.)

To fry samosas, heat about 1 to 1½ inches of oil in a deep pan to 360° on a deep-fat-frying thermometer. Add 4 or 5 samosas (freshly made, refrigerated, or thawed frozen) to oil; fry 1 to 2 minutes or until golden brown, turning to cook evenly. Lift from oil with a slotted spoon; drain on paper towels. Keep warm in a 200° oven until all are cooked. Serve warm.

Or cool, package airtight, and freeze. To reheat, place frozen samosas in a single layer on a shallow baking sheet and bake, uncovered, in a 350° oven for about 15 minutes or until hot.

Serve with Yogurt Sauce. Makes about 6 dozen appetizers.

Yogurt Sauce. Stir together 2 cups unflavored yogurt, ¼ cup finely chopped chutney, and 1 teaspoon crumbled dry mint flakes until well blended.

SEASONED POPCORN

Popcorn, an ever-popular snack, puts on a party dressing in this recipe.

    ¾ cup popcorn, unpopped
    ¼ cup melted butter or margarine
    1 clove garlic, minced or pressed, *or* 1 teaspoon paprika *or* ½ teaspoons onion salt *or* 2 tablespoons grated Parmesan cheese
    Salt

Pop popcorn as usual. Mix together butter and *one* of the seasonings: garlic, paprika, onion salt, or cheese. Pour butter on popcorn and toss; salt to taste. Makes 15 cups.

Cold
Appetizers
cool & refreshing make-ahead hors d'oeuvres

Chilled and crispy marinated vegetables, seasoned with aromatic spices, appear on the opposite page as a colorful and delightful change-of-pace appetizer. On the following 10 pages, you'll find recipes for these and many other cold appetizers made from vegetables, fruits, meats, and seafood.

Cold hors d'oeuvres are versatile and convenient. First of all, they can be made ahead by a well-organized host or hostess. Some of the hors d'oeuvre recipes even offer creative ways to utilize leftovers—cooked artichokes, green beans, carrots, eggs, and shrimp, for example.

Do-it-yourself oven-dried turkey, chicken, or beef jerky and salt-and-sugar-cured salmon (Swedish Salmon Appetizer) are two unusual recipes that guide you in making delicatessen-style foods at home. You'll be able to be extravagant with your servings, since the do-it-yourself method is relatively inexpensive.

If you're planning a large reception or tea, you'll want to study the feature called "Geometry and Sleight of Hand with Party Sandwiches" on page 63. It gives the secrets for making tiny sandwiches in the shapes of pinwheels, ribbons, and triangles.

For continental-style appetizers, turn to "Cheese with Fruit and Vegetable Accompaniments" on page 66. The classic combination of crisp, juicy produce with pungent and sometimes highly seasoned cheese is a delightful prelude to a meal.

Such recipes as Beef Tartare Rounds and Deviled Eggs round out the chapter. And to balance any hors d'oeuvre menu, we present suggestions for toasted and spiced nuts and seeds.

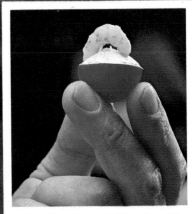

Stuffed Cherry Tomato Halves (page 59).

Chilled Marinated Carrots and Cauliflower,
Pickled Mushrooms, and Marinated Green
Beans make refreshing hors d'oeuvres.
(Recipes on page 58)

GINGER-MINTED CARROTS

(Pictured on page 73)

Mint-topped carrots marinated in a ginger-flavored orange juice mixture will be a favorite appetizer on hot summer days. Use whole baby carrots or cut large carrots into sticks.

- 3 **packages (10 oz. *each*) frozen baby carrots *or* about 2 pounds fresh baby carrots (peeled) *or* about 2 pounds large carrots (peeled and cut into ½ by 3-inch sticks)**
- 1 **cup orange juice**
- 1 **teaspoon grated fresh ginger Dash *each* salt and pepper**
- 1 **tablespoon chopped fresh mint**

In a pan, combine carrots, orange juice, ginger, salt, and pepper. Cover and bring to a boil; then reduce heat and simmer frozen carrots about 3 minutes, fresh carrots about 7 minutes, or until fork tender. Put carrots and their liquid in a bowl or container. Cover and chill at least 6 hours or as long as 1 week.

To serve, drain carrots and spoon into a bowl; garnish with mint. Serve with wooden picks. Makes about 6 cups.

MARINATED GREEN BEANS

(Pictured on page 57)

Calorie-watchers can enjoy these crisp, dill-flavored vegetable appetizers without concern. The marinade works well for carrots and cauliflower, too.

- 2 **pounds green beans Water**
- 3 **tablespoons coarse (kosher-style) salt**
- 2 **teaspoons *each* mustard seed and dill weed**
- 1 **teaspoon crushed small, dried, hot chile peppers**
- 1 **teaspoon dill seed**
- 4 **cloves garlic**
- 2 **cups white vinegar**
- ⅔ **cup sugar**

Snip ends from beans and wash thoroughly; leave whole or cut in half. In a large pan, bring 2 quarts water to a boil; add 1 tablespoon salt and beans. Return water to a boil and cook beans, uncovered, for about 5 minutes or until beans are just fork tender but are still bright green. Drain immediately and cool. Turn beans into a 2-quart bowl or container. Add mustard seed, dill weed, chiles, dill seed, and garlic.

In a small pan, combine 2 cups water, vinegar, sugar, and remaining 2 tablespoons salt. Bring to a boil over high heat; pour over beans. Cool slightly, cover, and chill at least 6 hours or as long as 2 weeks. Makes about 2 quarts.

Marinated Carrots. Follow directions for Marinated Green Beans, but substitute 2 pounds baby carrots (peeled) or 2 pounds large carrots (peeled and cut into thin sticks) for beans. Cook about 7 minutes or until fork tender.

Marinated Cauliflower. Follow directions for Marinated Green Beans, but substitute 2 pounds cauliflower (separated into flowerets) for beans. Cook 3 minutes or until flowerets are tender.

GARLIC OLIVES

Easy to make, these Italian-style olives should be prepared a day in advance to allow the olives time to soak up the spicy marinade.

- 3 **tablespoons olive oil**
- 1 **clove garlic, minced or pressed**
- ½ **teaspoon oregano leaves**
- 2 **cans (7 oz. *each*) pitted ripe olives, drained**

In a small bowl, stir together oil, garlic, and oregano. Add olives and toss to coat thoroughly with marinade. Cover and chill at least 4 hours or as long as 2 weeks. Makes about 1½ cups.

PICKLED MUSHROOMS

(Pictured on page 57)

These appetizers are made by layering mushrooms and onion slices in a piquant vinegar mixture.

- 3 **pounds small or medium-size mushrooms Water**
- 2 **medium-size white onions, thinly sliced**
- ½ **cup white vinegar**
- 1½ **teaspoons salt**
- ½ **bay leaf**
- ¼ **teaspoon whole black peppers**
- 1 **teaspoon olive oil**

In a pan, place mushrooms and 1 quart water. Bring to a boil; then reduce heat and simmer, uncovered, for about 15 minutes or until fork tender. Drain, reserving liquid. Place mushrooms and onions in layers in a 1-quart jar or container. In a pan, combine vinegar, mushroom liquid, salt, bay leaf, and pepper; bring to a boil; then reduce heat and simmer, uncovered, for 10 minutes; pour over layered vegetables. Add olive oil to jar, allowing it to float on top. Cover and chill for at least 24 hours or as long as 1 week. Offer wooden picks to spear vegetables. Makes about 1 quart.

CHERRY TOMATOES IN HERB MARINADE

These marinated and well-chilled tomatoes make a colorful addition to any hors d'oeuvre table.

    2 baskets cherry tomatoes
      Water
    ¼ cup red wine vinegar
    2 tablespoons instant minced onion or 2 green onions, sliced
    ½ teaspoon dry basil, crushed
    ¼ teaspoon oregano leaves, crushed
    1 teaspoon garlic salt
    ¼ teaspoon pepper
    ½ cup salad oil (may be part olive oil)

Put tomatoes, a few at a time, into a colander or wire strainer and dip into a large pan of boiling water for about 10 seconds. Immediately rinse tomatoes with cold water. Slip off peels and stems and put tomatoes into a bowl or container.

Stir together vinegar, onion, basil, oregano, salt, pepper, and oil until blended; then pour over tomatoes. Cover and chill for at least 2 hours or as long as 24 hours, stirring gently several times.

To serve, lift tomatoes from marinade with a slotted spoon. Provide wooden picks to spear tomatoes. Makes about 40 appetizers.

CHERRY TOMATOES WITH SMOKED OYSTERS

Fresh tomatoes and smoked oysters make an unusual flavor combination in these colorful and easy-to-make appetizers.

    2 baskets cherry tomatoes
    1 can (3 oz.) tiny smoked oysters, drained

Wash and stem tomatoes. Slice each tomato vertically to within about ¼ inch of base; spread apart and slip in a smoked oyster. Makes about 40 appetizers.

STUFFED CHERRY TOMATO HALVES

(Pictured on page 57)

Cut in half and stuffed, cherry tomatoes make neat, bite-size appetizers.

    1 basket cherry tomatoes
      Cheese and Shrimp or Guacamole Filling (recipes follow)

Wash and stem tomatoes; cut each in half crosswise. Scoop out seed pockets and discard. Lay cut side down on paper towels to drain about 30 minutes.

Make your choice of filling. With two spoons, pile about 1 teaspoon filling in each tomato half. Refrigerate as long as 4 hours if you wish. Garnish as directed and serve on a chilled plate. Makes about 40 appetizers.

Cheese and Shrimp Filling. In a small bowl, stir together 1 large package (8 oz.) cream cheese (softened), ¼ cup catsup, and 1 teaspoon dill weed until blended. Fill tomatoes with cheese mixture; garnish each with a small cooked shrimp (you'll need about 2 ounces altogether).

Guacamole Filling. Peel and remove pit from 1 large, ripe avocado. In a small bowl, mash avocado coarsely with a fork. Add 4 teaspoons lemon juice, 1 tablespoon finely chopped onion, 1 clove garlic (minced or pressed), and ½ teaspoon salt until blended. Fry 6 slices bacon until crisp; drain, cool, then crumble. Fill tomatoes with guacamole; garnish each with bacon bits.

MARINATED ARTICHOKE HEARTS

Packed in a spicy olive oil and vinegar marinade, these bite-size artichoke appetizers keep in the refrigerator up to a month.

    4 pounds small artichokes (*each about 2 inches in diameter*)
    6 tablespoons vinegar mixed with 2 quarts water
    1 cup *each* olive oil and white vinegar
    1 *each* whole carrot, small onion, and celery stalk
    2 cloves garlic
    1 stick cinnamon
    5 bay leaves
    ½ teaspoon *each* salt and whole black peppers

Slice off top third of each artichoke. Break off all coarse outer leaves down to pale inner leaves; peel stem. As artichokes are trimmed, dip in vinegar-water mixture for a few seconds to preserve color. Place in a large pan. Add oil, vinegar, carrot, onion, celery, garlic, cinnamon, bay leaves, salt, and whole peppers. Cover and bring to a boil, reduce heat, and simmer until tender (about 20 minutes). Let stand in liquid, covered, overnight.

Remove onion, bay leaves, and celery. Cut artichokes in half or leave very small ones whole. Return to marinade and bring to a boil. With slotted spoon, lift artichokes from liquid; arrange in 2 wide-mouth pint jars or in a bowl. To each pint, add 1 or 2 slices of the carrot, half the cinnamon stick, and 1 clove garlic. Bring remaining marinade to a boil. Pour over artichokes. Cover jars and refrigerate until well chilled or as long as 1 month.

To serve, transfer artichokes to a serving dish with a slotted spoon; offer wooden picks for spearing. Makes 2 pints.

For predinner appetizers, try Artichoke Sun-
burst with Cream Cheese Béarnaise, and
Ginger-spiced Prawns.
(Recipes on pages 61, 64)

FRESH ARTICHOKE APPETIZERS

(Artichoke Sunburst pictured on opposite page)

Both of these hors d'oeuvres begin with large artichokes, cooked in a lightly seasoned liquid and then chilled.

Artichoke Sunburst, a real showstopper, uses the heart of the artichoke as a cup to hold the dip for the surrounding leaves. For the dip, you can choose between a cold, tart hollandaise or a creamy béarnaise.

The Artichoke and Shrimp Appetizer uses the tender artichoke leaves as an edible platter for a shrimp-topped cream cheese mixture.

Artichoke Sunburst

- 1 large artichoke (at least 4 inches in diameter)
- 4 tablespoons vinegar
  Water
- 1 tablespoon olive oil or salad oil
- 1 bay leaf
- 2 whole black peppers
- ½ teaspoon salt
  Tart Hollandaise Sauce or Cream Cheese Béarnaise (recipes follow)

Slice about ½ inch off top of artichoke to remove main cluster of thorns; break off small leaves at base of artichoke and, with scissors, cut thorny tips from remaining exterior leaves. With a knife, cut away dark green surface of base and stem, trimming stem slightly.

Immerse artichoke in acidified water (3 tablespoons vinegar mixed with 1 quart water) for a few seconds to preserve color.

In a 2-quart pan, bring to a boil 1 quart water, the remaining 1 tablespoon vinegar, oil, bay leaf, peppers, and salt. Add artichoke, cover, return to a gentle boil, and cook about 45 minutes or until stem end pierces readily with a fork. Lift from cooking liquid, drain on paper towels, and let cool. Cut off stem; be sure base is flat so artichoke will sit upright.

To serve, pluck off leaves and lay them out on a platter in large,

overlapping rings. Discard tiny, filmy inner leaves; scoop choke from bottom and discard. Cut heart into thin wedges, holding it as you do so to retain cup form. Place heart in middle of leaves.

Mound heart area with Tart Hollandaise or Cream Cheese Béarnaise. Dip leaf base in sauce. Provide wooden picks to spear heart. Makes about 4 servings.

Tart Hollandaise Sauce. In a blender put 3 egg yolks, 3 tablespoons lemon juice, and ¼ teaspoon dry mustard. Whirl at high speed for about 30 seconds. Then gradually pour in ½ cup hot melted butter and add ¼ cup cold butter, cut in small pieces (a total of ¾ cup or ⅜ lb.). Whirl until smoothly blended, and serve.

Or cover and chill as long as 2 days. If sauce becomes too stiff, set container in warm tap water and stir constantly until desired consistency. Makes about 1 cup.

Cream Cheese Béarnaise. In a small pan, combine 2 tablespoons tarragon vinegar, 2 tablespoons minced green onion, and ¼ teaspoon tarragon leaves; bring to a boil over high heat and cook just until vinegar evaporates. Combine onion mixture, 2 small packages (3 oz. *each*) chive-flavored cream cheese (softened), ⅔ cup freshly grated Parmesan cheese, and 2 tablespoons lime juice until blended. Add about 2 tablespoons milk or cream to thin to a dipping consistency. Chill for at least 3 hours or as long as 4 days. Garnish with 2 tablespoons minced green onion. Makes about 1 cup.

Artichoke and Shrimp Appetizer

- 1 large artichoke (cut, cooked, and cooled as directed in preceding recipe)
- 1 small package (3 oz.) cream cheese
- ¼ teaspoon liquid hot pepper seasoning
- ½ teaspoon garlic powder
  Salt
  About 2 teaspoons half-and-half (light cream) or milk
  About ¼ pound small cooked shrimp
  Paprika

Stir together cream cheese, hot pepper seasoning, garlic powder, salt to taste, and cream until blended. Spread mixture on tip of each leaf, add a shrimp and sprinkle with paprika.

To serve, arrange leaves on a round plate or tray in shape of a sunflower. Makes about 30 appetizers.

ASSORTED ANTIPASTO PLATTER

Mixed antipasto plates, the favorite Italian prepasta hors d'oeuvre, can be a delightful way to begin a meal. You can make your antipasto platter as simple or as elaborate as you wish. Assemble the antipasto platter in advance or just before serving.

- ¼ to ½ pound butter or margarine, softened
- 1 or 2 cans (3 oz. *each*) sardines or 1 or 2 cans (2 oz. *each*) flat or rolled anchovy fillets
- 1 or 2 cans (about 6½ oz. *each*) white albacore tuna
- 1 or 2 jars (6 oz. *each*) marinated artichoke hearts
- 1 or 2 jars (6 oz. *each*) marinated mushrooms
- 1 or 2 baskets cherry tomatoes
- 1 or 2 small cans (8 oz. *each*) pitted ripe olives
- 1 jar (1 lb.) marinated garbanzo beans
- 1 to 1½ pounds cold meats (sliced dry salami, mortadella, Genoa-style salami, zampino, galantina, coppa, or a whole dry salami)
- 1 or 2 loaves French bread, sliced
- 1 pound or larger chunk jack or soft teleme cheese

To set up antipasto platter, put butter in a small bowl. Put individual fishes and vegetables in individual bowls. Arrange sliced meats and bowls of fish and vegetables on a large tray; place bread and cheese on a cutting board with a knife.

Invite guests to make up sandwiches of the fish, meat, cheese, and vegetables or pick up and eat individual foods. Makes about 6 to 12 servings.

JÍCAMA APPETIZER

A large tuberous root, jícama is a popular vegetable appetizer in Mexico. Typically it is peeled to serve raw with lime and a spicy salt mixture.

- 1 tablespoon salt
- ¼ teaspoon chile powder
- 1 lime
- 1 to 2-pound jícama

In a small serving bowl, combine salt and chile powder. Cut lime into wedges and place on serving dish. Peel jícama and cut into ¼ to ½-inch-thick slices. Place on a serving tray. To eat, rub lime over jícama, then dip into seasoned salt. Makes about 6 servings.

SPINACH SQUARES

Chilled and cut into small squares, this savory baked spinach mixture is firm enough to eat out of hand.

- 2 packages (10 oz. *each*) frozen chopped spinach
- 3 tablespoons butter or margarine
- 1 small onion, chopped
- ¼ pound mushrooms, sliced
- 4 eggs
- ¼ cup fine dry bread crumbs
- 1 can (10¾ oz.) condensed cream of mushroom soup
- ¼ cup grated Parmesan cheese
- ⅛ teaspoon *each* pepper, dry basil, and oregano leaves

Place spinach in a wire strainer, rinse under hot water to thaw, then press out all water; set aside. Melt butter in a frying pan over medium heat; add onion and mushrooms and cook, stirring, until onion is limp.

In a bowl, beat eggs with a fork; then stir in bread crumbs, mushroom soup, 2 tablespoons of the cheese, pepper, basil, oregano, drained spinach, and onion mixture until blended.

Turn into a well-greased 9-inch-square baking pan; sprinkle with remaining cheese. Bake, uncovered, in a 325° oven

for 35 minutes or until set when lightly touched. Cool slightly; then cover and refrigerate.

Cut into 1-inch squares and serve cold. Or reheat in a 325° oven for 10 to 12 minutes. Makes about 7 dozen appetizers.

BASIC DEVILED EGGS AND VARIATIONS

Crunchy, savory, and fishy stuffings are given here as variations on a familiar deviled egg theme.

- 6 hard-cooked eggs, shelled and halved lengthwise
- 3 tablespoons mayonnaise or sour cream
- ½ teaspoon dry mustard
  Dash cayenne or liquid hot pepper seasoning
  Salt
  Parsley sprigs or slices of green or ripe olives

Remove yolks from eggs and mash with a fork. Add mayonnaise, mustard, and cayenne, stirring until thoroughly blended. Stir in salt to taste. Fill 12 egg white halves evenly with egg yolk mixture. Garnish with parsley or olive slice.

Arrange eggs in a single layer in a deep dish; cover and refrigerate until eggs are chilled or until next day. Makes 12 halves.

Anchovy Celery Eggs. Follow basic deviled egg recipe but omit dry mustard and salt. Add 1 teaspoon anchovy paste and 6 tablespoons finely chopped celery to egg yolk mixture.

Crunchy Almond Eggs. Follow basic deviled egg recipe but omit mustard, cayenne, salt, and garnish. Add ¼ teaspoon garlic salt, 1 teaspoon Dijon mustard, and 3 tablespoons chopped salted roasted almonds to egg yolk mixture. Garnish with whole salted roasted almonds.

Oriental Eggs. Follow basic deviled egg recipe but omit mustard, cayenne, and salt. Add ½ teaspoon soy sauce, 2 tablespoons

finely minced green onion, and 3 tablespoons finely chopped water chestnuts to egg yolk mixture. Garnish with parsley sprigs.

Dilled Eggs. Follow basic deviled egg recipe, adding 2 tablespoons chopped dill pickle to egg yolk mixture.

Caviar Eggs. Follow basic recipe but omit mustard and garnish. Add 1 teaspoon lemon juice to egg yolk mixture. Garnish each egg half with ¼ teaspoon drained red or black caviar.

PARSLEY SHRIMP BALLS

Shrimp balls—made with Neufchâtel cheese, rolled in parsley, and adorned with tiny shrimp—are low-calorie hors d'oeuvres that are tasty enough to please non-calorie-counters, too.

- 10 ounces small cooked shrimp or 2 cans (5 oz. *each*) shrimp, drained
- 4 ounces Neufchâtel cheese, softened
- 3 tablespoons finely chopped celery
- 1 clove garlic, minced or pressed
- ¼ teaspoon liquid hot pepper seasoning
- 1 teaspoon soy sauce
  About ⅔ cup finely chopped parsley

Rinse and thoroughly drain shrimp; spread out on paper towels; pat dry. Set aside 40 whole shrimp for garnish; coarsely chop remaining shrimp.

In a bowl, beat together cheese, celery, garlic, hot pepper seasoning, and soy until very smooth. Stir in chopped shrimp just until blended. Cover and chill about 1 hour or until easy to handle.

Sprinkle parsley on a piece of wax paper. For each appetizer, shape 1 teaspoon cheese mixture into a ball, then roll in parsley to coat all sides. Spear reserved shrimp on wooden picks and stick one shrimp into each ball. Cover and refrigerate until thoroughly chilled or until next day. Makes about 40 appetizers.

GEOMETRY AND SLEIGHT OF HAND
WITH PARTY SANDWICHES

Here are the secrets for making tiny tea sandwiches with their unusual and intricate-looking layers and swirls.

The success of these sandwich loaves depends on uniformly sliced bread—best results are achieved with machine-sliced loaves. We recommend that you order bread baked in square-ended (or Pullman) loaves from a bakery. You can have the bread sliced horizontally or vertically. The following recipes are designed for loaves about 15 inches long, which yield about 40 vertical or 8 horizontal slices.

To make the sandwiches easier to prepare, freeze the loaves of sliced bread. When frozen, trim, fill with an appropriate spread from pages 17–23, and assemble; then package airtight and freeze.

On the day of the party, remove the sandwich loaves from the freezer. Unwrap loaves completely and let them stand, uncovered, to partially thaw. Then cut the loaves into individual sandwiches.

Arrange sandwiches attractively on serving trays; cover with clear plastic film and let thaw completely. You can refrigerate covered trays of sandwiches up to 3 hours before serving. Allow four to six sandwiches for each guest.

Ribbon Sandwiches
To make each 4-layer ribbon loaf, use 4 horizontally cut slices of bread, each about 15 inches long and ¼ inch thick. Trim crusts from frozen slices and spread each slice with about 4 teaspoons soft butter or margarine; butter both sides of slices that will be used in center of loaf.

Spread 3 of the slices with about ½ cup filling. Assemble loaf by stacking spread slices on top of each other; top with remaining slice of bread, buttered side down. Wrap each loaf in foil; package airtight and freeze.

To serve, unwrap and let stand until partially thawed and just easy to cut (about 45 minutes). Cut vertically in ½-inch-thick slices; then cut each section in half to make 2 sandwiches of 4 layers each. Arrange on trays, cover, and let thaw completely (about 30 minutes). Makes 60 small sandwiches.

Pinwheel Sandwiches
To make 2 pinwheel rolls, use 1 horizontally cut slice of white or whole-wheat bread, about 15 inches long and ¼ inch thick. Trim crust from frozen bread and spread slice with about 4 teaspoons soft butter or margarine; cover evenly with ½ cup filling. Cut slice in half crosswise and let stand until completely thawed (about 10 minutes). Roll each section from one narrow end in a jelly roll fashion. Wrap each roll in foil; package airtight and freeze.

To serve, unwrap and let stand until partially thawed and just easy to cut (about 40 minutes). Place each roll seam side down and cut in ⅓-inch-thick slices. Arrange on trays, cover, and let thaw completely (about 15 minutes). Makes 18 pinwheel sandwiches.

Triangular or Square Sandwiches
To make each large sandwich, use 2 vertically cut slices of frozen white or whole-wheat bread, each ¼ inch thick. Trim crusts from frozen bread and spread each slice with about 1 teaspoon soft butter or margarine; then spread 1 buttered slice with about 2 tablespoons filling and top with remaining bread slice, buttered side down. Wrap each in foil; package airtight and freeze.

To serve, unwrap and let stand until partially thawed and just easy to cut (about 20 minutes). For triangular sandwiches, cut each large sandwich from opposite corners, making an X. For square sandwiches, cut a large sandwich in half, then in half again. Arrange on trays, cover, and let thaw (about 15 minutes). Makes 4 sandwiches.

LIME AND PRAWN COCKTAIL

Hot pepper seasoning adds zest to this refreshing lime-based prawn sauce.

1½ pounds (about 45 count) medium-size prawns, cooked, shelled, and deveined
¼ teaspoon grated lime peel
¼ cup *each* lime juice and dry white wine
½ cup catsup
  Salt
3 or 4 drops liquid hot pepper seasoning

Place prawns in a deep bowl. Stir together lime peel and juice, wine, catsup, salt to taste, and hot pepper seasoning until blended; pour over prawns, tossing to coat thoroughly. Cover and chill at least 4 hours or until next day.

To serve, transfer prawns and several tablespoons of marinade to a serving dish. Provide wooden picks to spear prawns. Makes about 45 appetizers.

GINGER-SPICED PRAWNS

(Pictured on page 60)

For an elegant presentation, place cracked ice in a stemmed glass and arrange prawns around the lip of the glass.

To make the prawns go farther, cut them in half as you shell and devein them.

½ pound (8–10 count) large prawns
1 tablespoon finely chopped fresh ginger or ¾ teaspoon ground ginger
½ cup chopped green onion
1 teaspoon salt
1 teaspoon whole black peppers
  Water

In a small pan, put prawns, ginger, onion, salt, peppers, and enough water to barely cover prawns. Cover pan, bring to a boil, and boil gently for 3 to 4 minutes or until prawns turn bright pink. Let stand in stock until cool enough to handle. Remove prawns from stock, shell and devein, then return to stock.

Cover and refrigerate until chilled or until next day.

To serve, drain prawns and place on a small serving dish. Or, for each serving, place cracked ice in a stemmed glass and hang prawns around lip of glass. Makes 8 to 10 appetizers.

ICED SEAFOOD HORS D'OEUVRE

A bowl or tray of assorted seafood on cracked ice makes a dramatic display; it is particularly appealing on a hot summer day.

Cooked seafood (allow about ⅓ pound per person) such as prawns (shelled and deveined), chunks of lobster meat, clams and oysters in their shells, smoked oysters, squares of smoked sturgeon, rolls of smoked salmon, and chunks of finnan haddie
1 cup mayonnaise
¼ cup whipping cream, whipped
½ cup *each* tomato-based chile sauce, chopped green pepper, and minced green onion
  Salt
  Lemon juice
  Lemon wedges

Fill a large bowl or tray with cracked ice. Arrange a combination of seafood on ice. Spear seafood morsels (except those in shells) with wooden picks.

In a bowl, stir together mayonnaise, cream, chile sauce, green pepper, and onion until well blended. Add salt and lemon juice to taste, and stir until blended.

Nest bowl of dressing in ice and surround with lemon wedges. Makes about 2½ cups dip, enough for 3 to 4 pounds fish.

SWEDISH SALMON APPETIZER

This mild salmon appetizer that Swedes call *gravlax* resembles Jewish lox. A dill-seasoned mixture of salt and sugar lightly cures and firms the salmon overnight in the refrigerator.

12 to 15-inch salmon fillet (about 1½ to 2 lb.)
¼ cup *each* salt and sugar
1 teaspoon dill seed, crushed
  Garnishes (suggestions follow)

Rinse salmon and wipe completely dry. Carefully cut away any small bones on edges; with tweezers, pull out any small bones from center.

Place salmon, skin-side-down, in a flat-bottomed glass baking dish. Stir together salt, sugar, and dill seed. Sprinkle thickly on top of fish.

Cover and refrigerate for about 12 hours, turning fish occasionally. Several times during that period, pour off liquid that drains from fish. At end of 12-hour period, scrape any remaining salt mixture off fish.

To serve, cut fillet into thin, slanting slices just down to skin; discard skin. Serve salmon slices with cucumber slices, toast, pumpernickel or rye bread, or crackers. Offer a choice of seasonings: salt, freshly ground pepper, dill weed, chopped green onion, or fresh lemon. You could also offer sour cream, butter, or cream cheese to spread on bread or crackers. For best flavor, serve within 2 or 3 days. Makes 4 to 5 dozen appetizers.

PICKLED HERRING

Because it begins with prepared herring—refrigerated or canned—this traditional Swedish herring dish called *inlagd sill* goes together quickly.

Allow a minimum of ½ cup of herring per serving and offer with a bowl of sour cream.

1½ cups (or 2 jars, 6 to 8 oz. *each*) marinated or wine-flavored herring fillet pieces
1 carrot
1 small red onion
1 teaspoon whole allspice, slightly crushed
⅓ cup white vinegar
1 cup water
⅔ cup sugar
1 whole bay leaf

Drain liquid from herring; peel and thinly slice carrot and onion.

Alternate layers of herring, carrot, onion, and allspice in a deep container (4-cup capacity) until all ingredients are used. Stir together vinegar, water, and sugar; pour over herring. Tuck bay leaf into container. Cover and chill at least 24 hours or up to 4 days.

To serve, provide small plates and forks. Makes about 3 cups.

BEEF TARTARE ROUNDS

Raw egg yolk is the sauce for this typical Danish appetizer. For a unique presentation, serve the "sauce" from its own shell.

½ pound ground beef sirloin
¼ teaspoon garlic salt
¼ teaspoon tarragon (optional)
⅛ teaspoon pepper
  Salt
  About 3 medium-size onions
1 egg
  Butter
8 or 9 slices firm-textured pumpernickel bread

In a bowl, stir together sirloin, garlic salt, tarragon, pepper, and salt to taste. Cut onion in ¼-inch-thick slices; separate about 3 dozen inner bite-size rings (reserve rest for other uses).

Place small onion rings side by side on a serving tray; press into each ring about 1 teaspoon of the beef mixture. Cover and chill 2 hours or as long as 8 hours.

To serve, crack egg and put yolk in a shell half (reserve white for another use); set shell in an onion ring on serving tray. Butter bread; then cut in quarters. To serve, let guests lift an onion and beef round onto bread, spoon on a tiny portion of egg yolk, if desired, and eat. Makes about 3 dozen appetizers.

OVEN-DRIED JERKY

In this modern version of the ancient method of preserving meat, your oven, rather than the sun, dries the thin, seasoned strips.

Partially freezing the meat before cutting makes it easier to slice evenly. Cut with the grain of the meat if you like a chewy jerky; cut across the grain for a more tender, brittle product. Serve it as an appetizer with a mild cheese and fresh vegetables.

1½ to 2 pounds lean, boneless beef (flank, brisket, or round), venison, or chicken or turkey (white meat only)—partially frozen
¼ cup soy sauce
1 tablespoon Worcestershire
¼ teaspoon *each* pepper and garlic powder
½ teaspoon onion powder
1 teaspoon hickory smoke-flavored salt

Trim and discard all fat from meat. Cut meat into ⅛ to ¼-inch-thick slices (with or across grain—see above). If necessary, cut large slices to make strips about 1½ inches wide and as long as possible.

In a bowl, stir together soy, Worcestershire, pepper, garlic powder, onion powder, and smoke-flavored salt until blended.

Add meat strips and mix to coat thoroughly. Let stand at room temperature 1 hour or cover and refrigerate as long as 24 hours; meat will absorb most of liquid.

Shaking off any excess liquid, arrange strips of meat close together, but not overlapping, directly on oven racks or on cake racks set in shallow-rimmed baking pans.

Place meat in oven set at lowest possible temperature (150° to 200°). Bake until meat has turned brown, feels hard, and is dry to the touch (about 5 hours for chicken and turkey, 4 to 7 hours for beef and venison). Pat off any beads of oil. Let cool to room temperature; then remove from racks and store in an airtight container.

Keep at cool room temperature or in refrigerator until ready to use; keeps indefinitely. Makes about ½ pound.

SPINACH-WRAPPED CHICKEN WITH ORIENTAL DIP

Fresh spinach makes a handsome jacket for marinated chicken chunks. The tidy package is then dipped in a spicy sesame seed sauce.

2 whole (about 2 lb.) chicken breasts
1 can (14 oz.) regular-strength chicken broth
¼ cup soy sauce
1 tablespoon Worcestershire
1 bunch (1 lb.) fresh spinach
  Water
  Oriental Dip (recipe follows)

(Continued on next page)

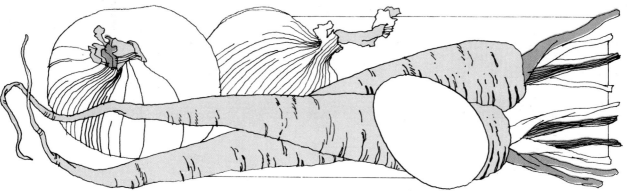

CHEESE WITH FRUIT AND VEGETABLE ACCOMPANIMENTS

The pure, clean tastes of cheese and fruit, when eaten together, make a welcome combination at almost any time of day. A more unusual but equally enjoyable match-up, though, is cheese and vegetables. Following are but a few of the cheese-with-fruit or cheese-with-vegetable pairs that naturally enhance each other. You might like to experiment and put together your own favorite combinations.

To serve, cut cheese, fruit, and vegetables into bite-size pieces (drizzle cut fruit with lemon juice to prevent darkening). Or set up a large wooden tray with wedges of cheese and whole fruits or vegetables in a basket. Provide cheese cutters and small sharp knives for do-it-yourself service.

Allow about ⅛ pound of cheese and about ½ to ¾ cup of fruits or vegetables for each appetizer serving.

Cheese	Fruits	Vegetables
Bel Paese	nectarines, peaches, apricots	green onions, edible pod peas
Blue, Gorgonzola, Stilton, Roquefort	apples, pears	fennel, cauliflowerets, carrot sticks
Brie	berries, papaya, mangoes	cucumber, mushrooms
Camembert	grapes, melon, berries	mushrooms, green beans
Cheddar	red-skinned apples	zucchini slices, cauliflowerets
Fontinella	Muscat grapes, Golden Delicious apples	broccoli flowerets, green beans
Havarti	peaches, nectarines	red pepper strips
Jarlsberg, Edam, Gouda	apples, pears, apricots	green peppers, tomatoes, mushrooms
Kuminost or Leyden	apples, pears	red and green pepper strips, tomatoes
Provolone	pineapple	edible pod peas, celery
Swiss, Emmenthaler, Gruyère	pears	asparagus spears, green beans
Teleme or jack	apricots, melons	cucumber slices
Tybo	Golden Delicious apples	mushrooms, cherry tomatoes

. . . Spinach-Wrapped Chicken (cont'd.)

In a pan, place chicken breasts, broth, soy, and Worcestershire. Bring to a boil, then simmer about 15 to 20 minutes or until fork tender. Lift chicken from broth and cool. Remove and discard skin and bones, then cut meat into 1-inch chunks.

Wash spinach thoroughly, remove and discard stems, and place leaves in a colander. Bring about 2 quarts water to a boil and pour over leaves; allow to drain thoroughly; set aside to cool.

To assemble, place a chunk of chicken at stem end of a large spinach leaf. Roll over once, fold leaf in on both sides, and continue rolling around chicken. Secure end of leaf with a wooden pick. Refrigerate until thoroughly chilled or until next day. Serve with Oriental Dip. Makes 50 to 60 appetizers.

Oriental Dip. Stir together ½ cup sour cream, 1 teaspoon toasted sesame seed, ¼ teaspoon ground ginger, 2 teaspoons soy sauce, and 1 teaspoon Worcestershire until blended. Refrigerate until chilled or until next day.

PINEAPPLE AND MANDARIN ORANGE APPETIZER WITH CURRY MAYONNAISE

(Pictured on page 73)

Serve this cool hors d'oeuvre during the summer months, when fresh pineapples are at their peak.

- 1 large fresh pineapple
- 1 can (11 oz.) mandarin orange segments
- ½ cup *each* mayonnaise and sour cream
- ¾ teaspoon grated orange peel
- 2 teaspoons curry powder
- 1 small clove garlic, minced or pressed

Reserving one half of shell, peel and core pineapple and cut into chunks. With a wooden pick, spear together a pineapple chunk and an orange segment; pile fruit kabobs into reserved pineapple shell. Cover and chill for 2 hours or until next day.

Stir together mayonnaise, sour cream, orange peel, curry powder, and garlic until blended. Cover and refrigerate until chilled or until next day.

To serve, place filled pineapple shell on a serving platter. Offer curry dip with fruit. Makes about 1 cup dip, 3 dozen fruit kabobs.

FRUIT WITH FLUFFY LIME TOPPING

Stiffly beaten egg white keeps this creamy topping fluffy. Serve it with your favorite fresh fruits.

- 2 cups strawberries
- 1 large papaya
- ½ fresh pineapple
- 1 cup whipping cream
- 3 tablespoons powdered sugar
- 1 teaspoon vanilla
- 2 teaspoons grated lime peel
- 1 egg white

Wash and hull strawberries; peel and seed papaya and cut into bite-size pieces; peel and core pineapple and cut into small chunks. Arrange fruits on a serving platter. Cover and chill up to 4 hours.

In a bowl, beat cream until soft peaks form; beat in powdered sugar, vanilla, and lime peel just until blended. Cover and chill up to 4 hours.

To serve, beat egg white until stiff (but not dry) peaks form; fold gently into cream just until blended. Pour into serving bowl to accompany fruit. Offer wooden picks for dipping. Makes about 2½ cups dip or about 10 servings.

NUT AND CHEESE-FILLED FRUITS

Enhance lichee nuts, kumquats, or grapes by giving them a Sherry-flavored filling.

- 1 small package (3 oz.) cream cheese, softened
- ⅛ teaspoon salt
- 1 tablespoon dry Sherry
- 2 tablespoons chopped nuts (walnuts, almonds, or macadamias)
- 1 can (1 lb. 4 oz.) lichee nuts, drained
  Parsley sprigs

Beat together cream cheese, salt, and Sherry until creamy and well blended. Stir in nuts.

Fill each lichee nut with about 1 teaspoon of the cheese mixture. Cover and refrigerate until thoroughly chilled or until next day. Garnish with parsley sprigs. Makes about 18 appetizers.

Filled Kumquats. Follow basic recipe but substitute 1 can (1 lb. 4 oz.) preserved whole kumquats (drained, cut in half, and seeded) or about 25 fresh kumquats (cut in half and seeded) for lichee nuts. Makes about 25 appetizers.

Filled Green Grapes. Follow basic recipe but substitute about 3 dozen seedless green grapes (cut in half) for lichee nuts. Makes about 3 dozen appetizers.

FLAVORED NUTS AND SEEDS

Roasted and flavored nuts and seeds make tasty appetizers or between-meal snacks.

- 1 cup shelled nuts such as almonds, pine nuts, peanuts, pecans, filberts, cashews, walnuts; dried seeds such as sunflower or soya; or rinsed fresh pumpkin or squash seeds
- 1 to 2 teaspoons salad oil
  Salt or seasonings (suggestions follow)

If using English walnuts, boil them in water to cover for 3 minutes; then drain and spread out on a towel to dry.

Spread nuts, dried seeds, or fresh seeds in a single layer in a shallow baking pan. Toast, uncovered, in a 350° oven until golden, stirring often. (Allow 8 to 10 minutes for almonds, pine nuts, peanuts, pecans, dried seeds, and blanched walnuts; 15 minutes for filberts and cashews; 40 minutes for rinsed fresh pumpkin and squash seeds.)

Drizzle with oil; season to taste with salt or stir in one of the seasoning blends (suggestions follow); return to oven for 2 to 3 minutes to blend flavors, stirring often. Let stand, uncovered, about 5 minutes to crisp or cool completely. Serve; or store in an airtight container up to 1 month.

Curry Seasoning. Combine 1 teaspoon curry powder, ½ teaspoon seasoned salt, and ⅛ teaspoon garlic powder.

Garlic Seasoning. Combine ½ teaspoon garlic salt and ¼ teaspoon *each* garlic powder and paprika.

Mexican Seasoning. Combine ¾ teaspoon chile powder, ½ teaspoon ground coriander, ¼ teaspoon *each* salt and ground cumin, and ⅛ teaspoon cayenne.

Oriental Seasoning. Use only 1 teaspoon salad oil; add 1 teaspoon sesame oil, 1 teaspoon Sansho Japanese pepper (or ½ teaspoon Chinese five-spice), salt to taste.

Smoky Seasoning. Combine ¼ teaspoon *each* smoke-flavored salt and seasoned salt, ⅛ teaspoon *each* garlic powder, onion powder, savory leaves, and cayenne.

Food and Wine Tasting Party is easy to assemble. Food stations free hostess and allow guests to serve themselves. From left to right: cheese, dessert, fish, and meat courses. For party plan, see page 78.

Party Menus

Nothing-to-it, Wine Tasting, Ethnic Themes

"Come to an appetizer party and plan to make it your dinner"—this should be the invitation to all the parties in this chapter. Each party offers many appetizer suggestions, along with ideas and recipes for beverages and desserts. You can follow each recipe plan for a complete party or choose from the list of suggested foods and make your party as simple as you like.

Most of the parties have menus that require little last-minute preparation and call for simple but smashing staging of food—such as the setting up of food stations as pictured on these two pages. This kind of plan, explained in the Nothing-to-it-Party (pages 70–71) makes any of the parties easy for the hosts to manage, easy for the guests to enjoy.

NOTHING-TO-IT PARTY

Effortless to give, a Nothing-to-It Party allows you to do large-scale entertaining in a limited space and to put out interesting fare with little preparation and few party props.

The physical arrangement of the party is what makes it work. Rather than staging a formal, sit-down affair with matching dinner service, you set up the individual courses at strategic and separate stations (indoors or outdoors), sufficiently close together to invite circulation, yet separate enough to avoid crowding.

The food, brought out just before the guests arrive, is kept at ideal serving temperatures and requires no attention once guests have arrived. It's ready to serve without plates and forks—all the food is hand-held.

Guests serve themselves in any order and at any rate that appeals to them, returning again and again to their favorites.

The following Nothing-to-It Party menus are four complete meals. You may wish to study the scheme of each, pick out ideas that will work for you, and then plan your party, adding your own variations. Or you may choose to prepare one of the complete Nothing-to-It Party menus.

Roast Beef Supper
or **Cold Turkey Dinner**
or **Baked Ham Dinner**
or **Pastrami Sandwich Supper**
(complete menus follow)

How to Present the Meal
All cooking (with the exception of the meat, if it is to be hot) is done ahead. You'll find it about as easy to serve three or four dozen guests as it is to serve one or two dozen if you follow these rules:
• Avoid any food that requires much individual attention, particularly at the last minute.
• Always let guests do as much of the serving as possible.
• When reasonable, keep foods whole or in large pieces; they look nicer and stay fresher.

• Have plenty of paper napkins and a waste receptacle at each station. Cleanup will be refreshingly brief and easy.

Apéritif. It's best placed quite near the entry. Guests serve themselves. Choose an apéritif wine, champagne, prepared punch, fruit juice, or any drink that needs no mixing.

Glasses. Allow one for each guest to use through the meal. If guests tend to be forgetful, give them name tags to attach to their glass. Use wine glasses (rent or borrow) or plastic throw-away cups.

Soup. It should be sippable and hot. Have either plastic or paper throw-away cups to hold the soup, and hot pads to protect hands if ladle or soup container is likely to get too hot to handle. Make your own favorite soup ahead or choose any good canned or dehydrated soup.

Meat. A large, visually attractive cut like a roast holds its flavor best, and leftovers are salvageable. If you wish to serve it cold, cook the meat the day before. Guests slice meat and make sandwiches; if you want a special bread, bake and freeze it, or order it from a bakery.

Wine. Offer just one kind for a whole meal; for comparison, you might serve the same varietal made by different wineries. Keep wine at a separate post.

Vegetable or salad. Dipping is the easy way to add sauce or dressing. Raw or cold cooked vegetables, kept mostly whole (thus easier to prepare) and attractively arranged, have a delightfully fresh look.

Dessert. Fruit, too, should be mostly whole and decoratively presented. Pears or apples to cut, pineapple cut in chunks and served from its shell, strawberries with stems all fit gracefully into this menu. Pair fruits with cheeses—large, handsome pieces from which guests do their own

cutting. As an alternate or an addition, offer a sweet that can be eaten out of hand, such as cookies or an uniced cake.

Coffee. This is easiest served from a large percolator urn. Make no apology about a miscellaneous collection of coffee cups—just tuck them into a picnic basket with buffers of colored tissue paper or napkins. Provide cream and sugar.

How to Calculate Quantities
Be generous in estimating the amounts of food and drink, as appetites can be surprising when guests have plenty of time and free rein. For example, for one serving, allow 1 cup of soup, about ½ pound of meat to make 3 or 4 sandwiches, a half bottle of wine, a big salad-size serving of vegetables, and fruit equal to the size of an apple.

COLD TURKEY DINNER

Station 1—Apéritif
Set out iced champagne to begin the meal. Continue with champagne or switch to a white wine, such as Sauvignon Blanc, Pinot Blanc, or Johannisberg Riesling. Use one large tub to hold all the bottles of wine.

Station 2—Soup
Present a pitcher full of clear homemade or canned mushroom soup. Keep soup warm over a flame, on an electric warming tray, or in an insulated jug.

Station 3—Entrée
Carve a few slices from a cold turkey and arrange around the bird, along with thinly sliced proscuitto (Italian-style ham). Accompany with prebuttered Parker House

rolls, kept warm on an electric warming tray.

Station 4—Vegetable
Group cold, cooked artichokes in a large bowl to eat leaf by leaf, dipping into room temperature hollandaise sauce (recipe on page 12). Provide a few spoons and knives for trimming hearts.

Station 5—Dessert
Serve cut pineapple in its shell; set out provolone cheese to slice and a jar of almond macaroons.

Finish with regular coffee or serve coffee royals. For the latter, allow 1 to 2 ounces whiskey, approximately 1 teaspoon sugar, and 1 lemon twist per cup.

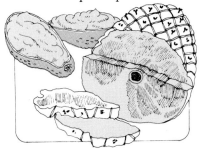

BAKED HAM DINNER

Station 1—Apéritif
Set out dry Sherry or other apéritif wines.

Station 2—Soup
Serve homemade or canned split pea soup from a tureen set on an electric warming tray, or from a soup pot on the kitchen range.

Station 3—Entrée
Serve ham hot or cold and tiny corn muffins hot or cold. If serving food warm, set on an electric warming tray. Accompany with a pot of butter and such relishes as chutney and watermelon pickles.

Station 4—Beverage
Choose either a chilled rosé or a mellow red wine, such as Chianti or Vino Rosso.

Station 5—Vegetables
Serve cherry tomatoes and homemade guacamole (recipe on page 11, pictured on page 9) or thawed, frozen avocado dip. (You might want to serve guacamole in avocado shells.) Provide tortilla chips for extra dipping and salt for nondipped tomatoes.

Station 6—Dessert
Serve seasonal fruit or Fruit with Fluffy Lime Topping (recipe on page 67) and thawed, frozen pound cake.

Finish with coffee.

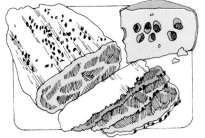

PASTRAMI SANDWICH SUPPER

Station 1—Beverage
For this sturdy fare, one beverage—such as a good, full-bodied Burgundy, or beer or ale—would do nicely throughout.

Station 2—Soup
For a warming preamble to the pastrami, serve strained onion soup or clear borscht in a punch bowl over the low heat of an electric warming tray.

Station 3—Entrée
Serve cold pastrami on a board with a wedge of Swiss cheese. Slice to serve on buffet-size rye bread. Offer pots of mustard, butter, and pickles.

Station 4—Vegetables
Accompany raw zucchini, Belgian endive, green beans, cabbage, and turnips with homemade or prepared mayonnaise. Have a knife at the table so vegetables can be cut off into bite-size pieces.

Station 5—Dessert
Serve fresh fruit, such as strawberries; accompany with powdered or granulated sugar for a dip. Set out slices of pound cake or spice cake.

Finish with regular coffee or Irish coffee. For the latter, nest bowl of whipped cream in ice; allow 1 to 2 ounces whiskey and 2 generous spoonfuls whipped cream per cup; float whipped cream on top.

ROAST BEEF SUPPER

Station 1—Apéritif
Set out dry Sherry, dry Vermouth, and Byrrh, with lemon twists and ice.

Station 2—Soup
Serve homemade stock or canned beef broth. Keep the soup warm in the fireplace, on the kitchen range or an electric warming tray, or over a flame.

Station 3—Entrée
Serve beef, roasted rare (140° or higher if you like), kept warm on electric warming trays. New York strip, cross-rib, or sirloin tip roasts (trimmed of excess fat) are all suitable boneless cuts. Meat should stay moist and tasty for about 6 hours. An electric knife is handy for cutting.

Embellishments for beef sandwiches, made on small round rolls, include sweet butter, lumpfish caviar, Dijon mustard, prepared horseradish, and a bouquet of watercress or curly endive in a vase of water.

Station 4—Beverage
Barbera is an appropriate choice, but any robust red wine will do.

Station 5—Salad
Set out inner leaves of romaine, small to medium-size raw mushrooms, and raw asparagus. For a dressing-dip, serve Green Goddess (recipe on page 12, pictured on page 9). Provide a knife for splitting vegetables.

Station 6—Dessert
Present a combination of Golden Delicious apples, a large chunk of Fontinella cheese, several small Danish Camemberts, and rich homemade or purchased cookies or pound cake. Set out a knife for guests to cut apples and cheese.

Finish with coffee.

PARTY WITH A FAR EASTERN FLAVOR

(Pictured on opposite page)

Present a party with an oriental flair by choosing a menu made up from a sampling of the following hors d'oeuvre recipes. Some are authentic oriental, Far Eastern, or South Pacific recipes; others are merely compatible with these or are oriental in feeling.

The recipes fall into specific categories; you'll want to study the categories and pick one or two appetizers from each for a well-rounded menu.

The party menu pictured on the opposite page shows only a small sampling of the great assortment of recipes listed. We served skewered Indonesian Chicken, Korean Beef Appetizers, Ginger-minted Carrots, Chinese Won Ton, Tofu Teriyaki Appetizers, Lumpia Appetizer with Dipping Sauce, Pineapple and Mandarin Orange Appetizer with Curry Mayonnaise, and purchased Chinese fortune cookies.

Dips with Chilled Vegetables and Crackers
Curry Dip (page 13; pictured on page 4)
Peanut Sauce (page 11)
Thai Chile Sauce (page 10)
Rumaki Spread (page 19)

Crab-Water Chestnut Appetizer (page 17)
Vegetable Suggestions: asparagus (cooked slightly), cauliflower, snow peas, carrots, mushrooms, Chinese cabbage, celery, cucumber, jicama, green pepper strips, green onion

Hot Fried Appetizers
Lumpia Appetizers (page 52)
Chinese Won Ton (page 54)
Spring Rolls (page 54)
Indian Samosas (page 55)

Main-dish Appetizers
Korean Beef Appetizers (page 45)
Water Chestnut Appetizers (page 43)
Chicken Wings Teriyaki (page 51)
Crispy Chicken Wing Appetizers (page 50)
Indonesian Chicken (page 51)
Spinach-wrapped Chicken with Oriental Dip (page 65)
Easy Rumaki or Japanese Rumaki (page 50)
Iced Seafood Hors d'oeuvre (page 64)
Almond Prawns (page 45)
Barbecued Prawns (page 46)
Tofu Teriyaki Appetizers (page 52)

Fruit and Vegetable Hors d'oeuvres
Pineapple and Mandarin Orange Appetizer with Curry Mayonnaise (page 67)

Ginger-minted Carrots (page 58)
Nut and Cheese-Filled Fruits (page 67)

Beverages
White wine, such as Gewurztraminer, Riesling, or Chardonnay
Lichee or Longan Punch (recipe follows)
Chinese or American beer
Iced tea

Dessert
Vanilla ice cream or orange sherbet topped with diced candied ginger or toasted coconut
Lichee nuts and canned mandarin oranges in their own syrup
Almond and fortune cookies

Lichee or Longan Punch

1 large can (1 lb. 4 oz.) lichees or longans
2 bottles (⁴/₅ qt. *each*) Emerald Riesling
4 teaspoons grenadine syrup
1 lime, thinly sliced

Combine lichees and their syrup with 1 bottle Emerald Riesling. Cover mixture and chill several hours or overnight.

To serve, add second bottle Emerald Riesling, grenadine, and lime slices. Ladle 1 or 2 pieces of fruit along with punch into each glass. Makes 12 servings.

FIESTA MEXICANA

Recreate the delightfully relaxed and charming atmosphere of Mexico with a south-of-theborder appetizer party. (Mexican cocktail-type parties are called *"el coctel"* and the appetizers *"antojitos"*—little whims.) Though most of the recipes listed here have been tempered slightly for less robust palates, they are based on authentic regional cooking of Mexico and South America (and can be spiced up to suit your taste).

For your party, assemble a menu with a sampling of recipes from each of the categories. You might use nachos as the hub of

the meal and, depending on the size of your group, add foods from the various categories.

Meat Hors d'oeuvres
Tamale Tempters (page 45)
Chorizo Tostadas de Harina (page 42)
Carne Seca Tostadas de Harina (page 42)
Appetizer Turnovers (page 35)

Seafood Hors d'oeuvres
Garlic Prawn Appetizers (page 45)
Lime and Prawn Cocktail (page 64)
Pastry Crab Puffs with Guacamole Dip (page 47)

Cheese Hors d'oeuvres
Tostadas de Harina (page 42)
Queso al Horno (page 42)

Nachos (page 15, pictured on front cover)
Chile con Queso (page 13)
Green Chile Cheese Dip (page 15)
Chiles-in-Cheese Fondue (page 26)

Vegetable Hors d'oeuvres
Guacamole (page 11)
Jicama Appetizer (page 62)

Dessert
Fruit with Fluffy Lime Topping (page 67)
Coffee ice cream with Kahlua on top

Beverages
Sangria (page 75)
Mexican or domestic beer
Carbonated apple juice
Iced tea or coffee

Party with a Far Eastern Flavor features (counter-clockwise from upper left) Indonesian Chicken and sauce, Korean Beef Appetizers, Pineapple and Mandarin Orange Appetizer with Curry Mayonnaise, Chinese Won Ton and dipping sauce, Lumpia Appetizers, Tofu Teriyaki Appetizers, purchased fortune cookies, Ginger-minted Carrots. For party plan, see opposite page.

SPIRITED LIQUID REFRESHMENT—HOT OR COLD

When planning party beverages, you can follow some general guidelines for estimating how much liquid you will need. Always consider the weather and your guest list when determining how much—and what—to buy.

For a 2½-hour-long party, allow about half a bottle of wine (white wine is more popular than red wine in summer; the reverse is true in winter) or champagne, 8 ounces of liquor, 1 quart of beer, or 16 ounces of mixed punch for each guest.

Another way to determine quantities is to figure that each drink you serve will last about 20 minutes. To judge how much to buy, multiply the number of 20-minute segments of the party by the number of guests.

Allow 2 quart bottles of nonalcoholic mix for each quart of liquor. A typical breakdown might be ⅓ soda, ⅓ tonic, and ⅓ assorted sweet mixes. In cool weather, soda is popular; in warm weather, tonic, orange juice, grapefruit juice, and water are preferred. You may want to provide other sweet carbonated mixes or a nonalcoholic punch (1 gallon will make about 32 servings).

Have on hand 1¼ pounds of ice per person (one 5-pound bag for four persons, one 50-pound bag for every 40 persons). You will also need napkins (at least two per person) and miscellaneous supplies such as fruit garnishes, stirrers, corkscrews, and bottle openers.

Unless you have name tags to attach to glasses, plan two per person. Plastic glasses, available in assorted shapes and sizes, can be great timesavers. If you prefer nonplastic glasses, consider renting or borrowing them from the shop where you purchase your wine or liquor.

Here we've included a selection of hot and cold punch recipes and apéritifs that are well suited to a variety of entertaining occasions.

Apéritifs

Apéritif drinks vary according to country, personal preference, and what is currently in vogue. But those most widely favored are the aromatic wines: the vermouths, the European apéritif wines, and the products of the United States officially designated as "special natural flavored wines."

> Well-chilled aromatic wines, such as Byrrh, Chambraise, dry or sweet vermouth, Dubonnet (red or blonde), Golden Spur, Lillet, Positano, Vive Italiano, Volare.
> Chilled soda water
> Ice cubes
> Lemon wedges

On a serving table, place one or more bottles of your choice of aromatic wines with a bottle of chilled soda water, a bucket of ice cubes, a bowl of lemon wedges, and wine or cocktail glasses.

To serve, put 1 or 2 ice cubes and a lemon wedge in a glass; fill glass with aromatic wine and soda water to taste.

French Kir

A frosty wine punch, French Kir is cool and refreshing and quick to make. It pairs a dry white wine with crème de cassis, a black currant liqueur. You might compare a kir to an apéritif, for it makes a fine predinner beverage.

> 1 bottle (⁴/₅ qt.) light fruity white wine (such as Chenin Blanc, Gewurztraminer, or Emerald Riesling), chilled
> ¼ to ½ cup crème de cassis
> Lemon peel
> Ice cubes

In a pitcher, combine wine and crème de cassis (amount depending on your own taste).

To serve, place a twist of lemon peel in an 8 to 10-ounce wine glass, add 2 ice cubes, and pour in about ½ cup wine-cassis mixture. Makes about 3½ cups or 7 servings of ½-cup size.

Sangría de Granada

A refreshing wine and fruit juice blend, sangría is a favorite Spanish punch. This version is authentic enough to be served within the rose and wisteria-covered walls of the Alhambra.

    1 medium-size orange
    ¼ cup sugar
    2 cups fresh orange juice
    1 bottle (⁴/₅ qt.) dry red wine
    ½ cup Cointreau (or other orange-
       flavored liqueur)

Cut orange in half. Cut 1 or 2 thin slices from one half, then cut each slice in quarters and save for garnish.

With a vegetable peeler, cut off thin outer peel of other half of orange. In a bowl and using a spoon, bruise peel with sugar to release flavorful oils; then stir in orange juice, wine, and Cointreau. Cover and chill; after first 15 minutes, remove orange peel.

To serve, pour sangría into a punch bowl or pitcher. Garnish with orange slices. Serve with ice, if desired. Makes 9 servings of ½-cup size.

Flaming Glögg

Welcoming and warming, a cup of spiced wine punch called *glögg* is a Scandinavian tradition that suits holiday festivities. You warm the liquid in the kitchen, then bring it out before guests to flame, ladling the blazing punch over melting sugar cubes.

    1 bottle (⁴/₅ qt.) dry red wine
    1 cup dry Sherry
    1 cup vodka
    10 to 15 whole cloves
    1 cinnamon stick
       About ⅔ cup sugar cubes
       About ¾ cup *each* raisins and whole
       almonds

In a 3-quart pan or kettle, combine wine, Sherry, vodka, cloves, and cinnamon. Place over medium heat until hot enough to sip; do not boil.

Remove from heat and present for flaming before your guests (do not set pan beneath an exhaust fan or anything that can catch fire). To flame, mound as many sugar cubes as possible in a slotted spoon or ladle and dip quickly into glögg. Lift out at once; hold a lighted match close to surface of punch to set aflame, then spoon glögg frequently over cubes to melt sugar and maintain flame (agitating the liquid releases alcohol fumes that burn). Add any remaining sugar to ladle and melt by same technique, or stir into glögg.

You can serve glögg as it flames; keep it warm on an electric warming tray or over a candle until all is served. Add a few raisins and almonds to each cup. Makes 10 servings of ½-cup size.

Frothy Eggnog Punch

Traditional holiday fare, this airy-textured eggnog can be prepared several hours ahead of your guests' arrival.

    14   eggs, separated
    1¼   cups sugar
    1   quart milk
    1   cup *each* whipping cream, rum, and
         brandy

Beat egg yolks until light and lemon-colored. In a 2-quart pan, combine yolks, ¾ cup of the sugar, and ¾ cup of the milk. Place over medium-low heat and cook, stirring constantly, for about 12 minutes or until mixture thickens to a soft custard; cool.

In a large mixing bowl, beat egg whites until frothy; gradually add remaining ½ cup sugar and beat until soft peaks form. In a 4-quart punch bowl, fold together cooled custard and beaten egg whites until blended.

Whip cream; then gently fold and stir cream and remaining 3¼ cups milk into egg white mixture just until blended. Refrigerate until thoroughly chilled (at least 2 hours).

Before serving, stir in rum and brandy. Makes 24 servings of 1-cup size.

Aegean Buffet features (clockwise from upper left) fresh fruit; halvah; pumpkin seeds; Skewered Dolmathes, Olives, and Eggplants; Hommus with Tahine surrounded by Greek olives; kasseri and feta cheeses; sweet French bread; Stuffed Clams; Cherry Tomatoes with Marinated Shrimp and Artichokes.

ALL-APPETIZER AEGEAN BUFFET

(Pictured on opposite page)

Our midsummer garden party captures the carefree nature of an Aegean appetizer buffet. The following menu, made up of dishes able to sit outdoors awhile without losing their flavor, will treat two dozen guests to a nonstop appetizer-through-dessert buffet. For our gathering we selected an array of dishes from the menu. The foods are authentically Greek, with a nod or two to the Turks, who, after all, influenced much of the Hellenic cuisine.

Greek specialty markets and international delicatessens carry many of the foods, such as fila (paper-thin dough), cheeses, olives, canned *dolmathes* (stuffed grape leaves—sometimes spelled *dolmades* or *dolmas*), baby eggplant, *tahine* (ground sesame seed), *baklava*, and *halvah* (sesame seed candy).

Aside from the main buffet, you might set out pumpkin seeds (allow ½ pound) and chunks of kasseri and feta cheese (1½ pounds *each*) for snacking.

To complement the food, we suggest serving authentic Greek wines and oúzo, the potent aniseed-flavored liqueur. Domestic California red and white *retsinas* (with their pitch-pine flavoring) are surprisingly inexpensive, yet compare favorably with Greek resinated wines. For a milder touch, try a California Pinot Blanc. Among Greek nonresinated wines, look for Hymettus (dry white), Roditys (rosé), or Kokineli (red).

For a finale make Turkish coffee (following directions on container) over a small brazier or hibachi on the spot. Also serve regular coffee brewed in the kitchen. Offer an abundance of fresh strawberries with stems (about 2 quarts), and 4 or 5 cantaloupes, cut into flower shapes, with seeds scooped out.

If it's available, buy chocolate-marbled halvah with nuts and offer honey-soaked baklava.

Sweet French Bread
Hommus with Tahine (recipe on page 17)
Cheese-filled Diamonds (recipe on page 31)
Meat-filled Fila Triangles (recipe on page 38)
Stuffed Clams (recipe follows)
Meatballs Oregano (recipe follows)
Cherry Tomatoes with Marinated Prawns and Artichokes (recipe follows)
Skewered Dolmathes, Olives, and Eggplants (recipe follows)
Pumpkin Seeds
Kasseri and Feta Cheeses
Cantaloupe and Strawberries
Baklava
Halvah
Turkish Coffee

Stuffed Clams (*Kidonia yemista*)
Heat ½ cup olive oil in a large frying pan over medium heat; add 1½ cups short grain (or pearl) rice; 2 medium-size onions, finely chopped; and ½ cup pine nuts. Cook, stirring, until nuts turn golden. Remove from heat.

Thoroughly drain and measure liquid from 3 cans (7½ oz. *each*) minced clams (if needed add enough water to make 1½ cups liquid) and pour over rice mixture. Stir in ½ cup tomato sauce, ½ teaspoon *each* dill weed and allspice, and ⅓ cup currants. Cover and let stand 30 minutes.

Bring to a boil over high heat, reduce heat to low, and let simmer precisely 12 minutes. Remove from heat and let stand (without removing cover) for 10 minutes. Add clams and stir lightly with a fork. Let cool slightly, then spoon into small shells, such as clam, mussel, or scallop shells (without shells, mound in a bowl). Chill, or freeze, well wrapped. Serve cold (thaw if frozen) with lemon wedges. Fills 4 dozen shells.

Cherry Tomatoes with Marinated Prawns and Artichokes (*Garides me Anginares Marinata*)
Cook, shell, and devein 5 pounds large (about 15 to a pound) prawns.

Drain marinade from 4 jars (6 oz. *each*) marinated artichoke hearts into a bowl and stir in ½ cup lemon juice and ½ teaspoon tarragon. Add prawns and stir lightly to coat; cover and chill.

To serve, arrange prawns down center of a platter; place artichoke hearts on one side and about 2½ cups cherry tomatoes on other side. Spoon marinade over shrimp. Makes about 24 servings.

Skewered Dolmathes, Olives, and Eggplants
Use 2 dozen 9-inch-long wooden skewers. Open 1 jar (about 1 lb.) stuffed small eggplants or cocktail eggplants and 2 cans (about 13 oz. *each*) dolmathes. Have on hand 4 dozen large Greek black olives or pitted California ripe olives.

Alternate on each stick a dolmathe, olive, eggplant, olive, and dolmathe. Poke into a large "frog" (the kind used for flower arranging) and stuff the metal base with parsley sprigs. Place on a small plate. Makes about 2 dozen skewered relishes.

Meatballs Oregano (*Keftethakia*)
Crumble 6 slices white bread and soak for 5 minutes in 1 cup milk; beat with a fork until mushy. Cook 1 cup finely chopped onion in 2 tablespoons butter until golden.

In a large mixing bowl, place 4 pounds lean ground beef, ¾ cup finely chopped parsley, 4 egg yolks, the milk mixture, onion, 4 teaspoons salt, and ¼ teaspoon pepper; thoroughly mix with your hands. Shape into 1¼-inch balls and place on two 10 by 15-inch baking pans. Bake in a 450° oven for 15 minutes or until meatballs are browned and slightly pink in center.

Meanwhile, bring ¾ cup red wine vinegar and 1 teaspoon oregano to a boil, reduce heat, and simmer 10 minutes; pour mixture over hot meatballs (half in each pan), scraping up pan juices. Serve immediately.

Or leave in pan, cover, and chill or freeze. To reheat (thaw if frozen), place in a 375° oven for 15 minutes. Makes about 6 dozen.

FOOD AND WINE TASTING PARTY

(Pictured on pages 68–69)

The intent of this informal party is twofold: to offer a limited sampling of wines and to reveal the character of each wine more clearly by serving it with complementary food.

You combine the wine and food along the lines of a several-course dinner, but you sidestep the demands of a sit-down meal. Each course, arranged at a separate station, is ready for guests to serve themselves. Once the party starts, the hosts need give no further attention to food preparation—they can relax and enjoy the party.

Unlike the courses of a dinner, these can be sampled in any order, and the stations can be revisited at any time.

Though the group can number as few as a dozen persons, you can serve two or three times that number with surprisingly little difference in effort.

The Food and Wine. Allow the same quantities of food as you would for a sit-down meal, and about half a bottle of wine and one glass for each person.

Between courses, each guest swirls a few drops of the new wine in his glass to rinse it.

Prepare cooked dishes ahead. When necessary, keep them warm or reheat to serve; use your chafing dishes, candle warmers, or electric warming trays.

All the foods we suggest can be eaten out of hand.

You can serve the exact four courses of fish, meat, cheese, and dessert listed here, or use any of the alternate choices described.

The Logistics. For a smooth-flowing party, the stations should be sufficiently close together to permit easy circulation, yet far enough apart to avoid crowding. Some seating should be provided. The size of table for each course needs to be large enough to accommodate only the food and wine. Our tables, covered with brightly colored felt tablecloths, were 24 inches in diameter.

Fish and chilled white wine (suggestions follow)
Meat and room-temperature red wine (suggestions follow)
Cheese and room-temperature red wine (suggestions follow)
Dessert and selected wines (suggestions follow)

Fish and Chilled White Wine
Sauvignon Blanc served with smoked salmon (Smoked Salmon, recipe on page 44, or Barbecued Salmon, recipe on page 40; or order at a fish market) and cucumber on buttered dark bread.
Alternate Courses
• Pinot Chardonnay with raw oysters on half shells (see Iced Seafood Hors d'oeuvre, page 64).
• Johannisberg Riesling with cooked shrimp on ice (Ginger-Spiced Prawns, page 64) or cold chunks of cooked lobster in shells to dip in bubbling butter and eat on sliced French bread.
• Sylvaner with hot scallops to spear from chafing dish.

Meat and Room-Temperature Red Wine
Cabernet Sauvignon and Red Wine Simmered Beef Cubes (recipe on page 45) to eat on sliced French bread, or small chunks of barbecued or broiled steak to spear.

Alternate Courses
• Gamay with lamb stew simmered in a red wine.
• Grignolino with hot, meat-topped mini-pizzas (see mini-breads, page 36).
• Ruby Cabernet and hot pork link sausages, tiny corn muffins.

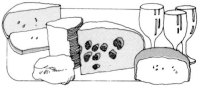

Cheese and Room-Temperature Red Wine
(Pictured on page 1)

Barbera with water crackers and Fontina, Oregon blue, Jarlsberg, and rondelé; *or* Gorgonzola, provolone, Reblochon cheeses; *or* Fresh Creamy Cheese (recipe on page 19); *or* Nut-studded Appetizer Cheeses (recipe on page 22).
Alternate Courses
• Zinfandel with bread sticks and Asiago, Fontinella, Samsoe.
• Pinot Noir with unsalted crackers, toasted almonds, and Brie, Camembert, or Le Beau Pasteur (French process cheese). Or omit nuts and offer Gorgonzola, Mycella, or Roquefort.
• Petite Sirah with plain wafers and Caerphilly.

Dessert and Selected Wines
Chilled fruity white wine such as a sweet Chenin Blanc, a white muscat type such as Muscato di Amabile, or Muscato di Canelli, Malvasia Bianca (12 percent), and butter cookies with a basket of fresh fruit such as strawberries, cherries, apricots, or other small seasonal fruits.
Alternate Course
• Chilled Haut (sweet) Sauterne, chilled Brut or Extra Dry Champagne, or room-temperature Tawny or Ruby Port with uniced pound cake and strawberries or nuts in shells.

Index

A

All-appetizer Aegean buffet, 77
Almond-Cheddar ball, 23
Almond prawns, 45
Anchoiade Provençal, 10
Anchovy, 10, 12, 14, 62
Anchovy celery eggs, 62
Antipasto platter, 61
Apéritifs, 74
Appetizers from the barbecue, 40
Appetizer turnovers, 35
Armenian hommus, 17
Artichoke, 39, 41, 59, 61, 77
Artichoke and shrimp appetizer, 61
Artichoke nibbles, 39
Artichoke sunburst, 61
Assorted antipasto platter, 61
Avocado, 11, 20
Avocado dip with red and black caviar, 11

B

Bacon and cottage cheese dip, 12
Bacon-wrapped prawns, 46
Bagels, mini, 36
Bagna cauda, 14
Baked chicken livers with mustard sauce, 50
Baked ham dinner, 71
Balancing the menu, 6
Barbecue, appetizers from the, 40
Barbecued prawns, 46
Barbecued salmon with biscuits, 40
Basic deviled eggs and variations, 62
Bean dip, 11
Beans, green, marinated, 58
Béarnaise, 25, 61
Beef, 25, 45, 65, 71
Beef, ground
    appetizer turnovers, 35
    beef tartare rounds, 65
    filling, for Chinese won ton, 54
    filling, for spring rolls, 55
    Indian samosas, 55
    Korean meatballs, 43
    meat-filled triangles, 38
    meat-filled turnovers, 34
    picadillo pastries, 34
    super nachos, 15
Beef tartare rounds, 65
Beverages, 72, 74–75
Biscuits, cocktail baking powder, 37
Blender hollandaise, 12
Bottomless cheese crock, 20

C

Calculating quantities
    beverages, 74
    food, 6, 66, 70
Camembert or Brie with almonds, 22
Camembert spread, 20
Caraway roll, 23
Carrots, 58
Cauliflower, marinated, 58
Caviar, 11, 62
Cheddar fondue appetizer cubes, 41
Cheddar tarts, 30
Cheese
    balls, 23, 41
    dip, 12, 15, 48
    fondues, 25–27, 41
    grilled, 40
    log, 33
    pastries, 31
    rounds, 47
    spreads, 17, 20, 22–23
    sticks, 34
    stuffings, 59, 67
    tarts, 30
    turnovers, 35, 38

Cheese and caraway appetizers, 34
Cheese and seed nibbles, 33
Cheese and shrimp filling, 59
Cheese-filled diamonds, 31
Cheese with fruit and vegetable accompaniments, 66
Cheese spritz, 31
Cheese straws, 33
Cherry cheese with almonds, 22
Cherry tomatoes, 59, 77
Cherry tomatoes in herb marinade, 59
Cherry tomatoes with marinated prawns and artichokes, 77
Cherry tomatoes with smoked oysters, 59
Chicken, 35, 50–51, 65
Chicken livers, 18, 50
Chicken wings teriyaki, 51
Chile, 10, 13, 15, 25, 38
Chile con queso, 13
Chile-in-cheese fondue, 26
Chinese won ton, 54
Chutney sauce, curried, 25
Clams, 10, 18, 47, 64, 77
Clams or oysters casino, 47
Classic Swiss fondue, 27
Cocktail baking powder biscuits, 37
Cocktail cream puffs, 37
Cold turkey dinner, 70–71
Cool and refreshing appetizer molds, 20
Crab, 11, 47
Crab and cheese rounds, 47
Crab and water chestnut spread, 17
Crab-stuffed mushrooms, 39
Cottage cheese and bacon dip, 12
Cream cheese béarnaise, 61
Cream cheese trio, 20
Cream puffs, cocktail, 37
Creamy Parmesan fondue, 25
Creamy pâté, 18
Crisp-baked artichoke appetizers, 41
Crispy chicken wing appetizers, 50
Crunchy almond eggs, 62
Cucumber chile dip, 13
Curried chutney sauce, 25
Curry dip, 13
Curry mayonnaise, for fruit, 67
Curry seasoning, for nuts and seeds, 67

D

Deep-fried crab puffs, 47
Deviled eggs, 62
Dilled eggs, 62
Dill-onion dip, 12
Dill tuna mold, 17
Dips, 10–16
Dips from the sea, 10
Dolmathes, skewered, 77

E

Easy, never-fail fondues, 26
Easy rumaki, 50
Eggplant, 13, 17, 77
Eggplant spread, 17
Eggs, deviled, 62
Empanadillas, 35

F

Falafil, 51
Fiesta Mexicana, 72
Fila dough, 31, 38
Filled green grapes, 67
Filled kumquats, 67
Filled lichee nuts, 67
Flaming glögg, 75
Flavored nuts and seeds, 67
Fluffy lime topping with fruit, 67

Fondues, 24–28, 41
Fonduta, 27
Food and wine tasting party, 78
Freezer cheese balls, 23
Freezer cheese sticks, 34
Freezing, 7
French kir, 74
Fresh artichoke appetizers, 61
Frothy eggnog punch, 75
Fruits, 66, 70–72, 77, 78
    grapes, 67
    kumquats, 67
    lichee nuts, 67, 72
    mandarin orange, 67
    pineapple, 67
Fruit with fluffy lime topping, 67

G

Garlic-herb cheese, 23
Garlic olives, 58
Garlic prawn appetizer, 45
Garlic seasoning, for nuts and seeds, 67
Ginger-minted carrots, 58
Ginger-spiced prawns, 64
Glazed sausage balls, 43
Glögg, flaming, 75
Grapes, cheese-filled, 67
Green beans, marinated, 58
Green chile cheese dip, 15
Green goddess dip, 12
Guacamole, 11
Guacamole filling, 59

H

Ham and papaya pupus, 42
Ham filling, for spring rolls, 55
Happy hour mushrooms, 39
Hasty hots, 41
Hearty appetizer meatballs, 42
Herbed cheese with nuts, 22
Herring, pickled, 64
Hollandaise sauce, 12, 61
Hommus, 17
Horseradish sauce, 43
Hot butter-oil sauce, 14

I

Iced seafood hors d'oeuvre, 64
Indian samosas, 55
Indonesian chicken, 51
Italian-style fondue, 26
Italian-style grilled sausage and cheese, 40

J

Japanese rumaki, 50
Jerky, oven-dried, 65
Jicama appetizer, 62

K

Kir, French, 74
Korean beef appetizers, 45
Korean meatballs, 43
Kumquats, cheese-filled, 67

L

Lamb meatballs, 42
Lemon almond scallops, 46
Lichee nuts, filled, 67
Lichee or longan punch, 72
Lime and prawn cocktail, 64
Liver pâté, 18
Liverwurst pâté, 19
Lumpia appetizers, 52

M

Mandarin orange and pineapple appetizer with curry mayonnaise, 67
Marinated artichoke hearts, 59
Marinated carrots, 58

Marinated cauliflower, 58
Marinated green beans, 58
Marinated onion, 26
Marinated water chestnut appetizers, 43
Meat and seafood fondue appetizer, 25
Meatballs, 42–43, 77
Meat-filled fila triangles, 38
Meat-filled turnovers, 34
Menu planning, 6
Mexican seasoning, for nuts and seeds, 67
Miniature chile-cheese turnovers, 38
Mini-bagels, 36
Mock béarnaise sauce, 25
Molded avocado cream, 20
Molded chicken liver pâté, 18
Molds, cool and refreshing appetizer, 20
Moroccan eggplant dip, 13
Mushrooms, 14, 38, 39, 58
Mushrooms with ham and artichokes, 38
Mustard dip, 47
Mustard sauce, 50

N

Nachos, 15
Nothing-to-it party, 70–71
Nut and cheese-filled fruits, 67
Nuts and seeds, flavored, 67
Nuts, to toast, 22
Nut-studded appetizer cheeses, 22

O

Olive-filled cheese balls, 41
Olives, 58, 77
Onion-dill dip, 12
Onions, marinated, 26
Oriental dip, 66
Oriental eggs, 62
Oriental seasoning, for nuts and seeds, 67
Oven-dried jerky, 65
Oysters, 17, 47, 59

P

Pacific crab dip, 11
Papaya and ham pupus, 42
Parmesan-garlic artichokes, 39
Parmesan pocket bread appetizers, 41
Parsley shrimp balls, 62
Party menus, 68–78
Party with a Far Eastern flavor, 72
Pastrami sandwich supper, 71
Pastries, 30–31, 33–38, 47
Pastry crab puffs, 47
Pastry shell, 30
Pâté, 18–19
Peanut sauce, 11
Pepperoni pizza appetizers, 36
Picadillo pastries, 34
Pickled herring, 64
Pickled mushrooms, 58
Pineapple and mandarin orange appetizer with
    curry mayonnaise, 67
Pinwheel sandwiches, 63
Pizza appetizers, pepperoni, 36
Pocket bread appetizers, 41
Popcorn, seasoned, 55
Pop-open barbecue clams, 40
Pork
    bacon and cottage cheese dip, 12
    bacon-wrapped prawns, 46
    filling, for Chinese won ton, 54
    filling, for spring rolls, 54
    glazed sausage balls, 43
    ham and papaya pupus, 42
    lumpia appetizers, 52
    marinated water chestnut appetizers, 43

Pork (cont'd)
    mushrooms with ham and artichokes, 38
    spicy sausage balls, 43
    tamale tempters, 45
Prawns, 45–46, 64, 77. See also Shrimp
Puffy cheese appetizers, 31
Punch, 72, 74–75
Pupus, 42

Q

Quantities, calculating
    beverages, 70, 74
    food, 6, 66, 70
Queso al horno, 42
Quiche Lorraine appetizer, 30
Quiche, shrimp, 30
Quick pastry twists, 33

R

Raclette, 26
Red wine simmered beef cubes, 45
Refried bean dip, 11
Ribbon sandwiches, 63
Roast beef supper, 71
Roquefort and sour cream dip, 12
Rumaki, 19, 50

S

Salami and cheese turnovers, 35
Salmon, 18, 44, 53, 64
Samosas, Indian, 55
Sandwiches, 63
Sangría de Granada, 75
Sausage, 40, 54
Sausage balls, 43
Savory stuffed mushrooms, 38
Scallops, lemon almond, 46
Schloss or blue cheese with walnuts, 22
Seafood, 25, 64
    anchovies, 10, 12, 14, 62
    clams, 10, 18, 47, 64, 77
    crab, 11, 17, 39, 47
    herring, 64
    oysters, 17, 47, 59
    prawns, 45–46, 64, 77
    salmon, 18, 44, 53, 64
    scallops, 46
    shrimp, 10, 30, 35, 54, 61, 62
    tuna, 17, 48, 61
Seasoned popcorn, 55
Seeds, 33, 67
Sesame cheese wafers, 33
Sesame seed, how to toast, 20
Shallot cream cheese with nuts, 22
Shrimp, 35, 54, 61, 62. See also Prawns
Shrimp and artichoke appetizer, 61
Shrimp dip, 10
Shrimp quiches, 30

Skewered dolmathes, olives, and eggplants, 77
Smoked oyster and cheese spread, 17
Smoked salmon from the barbecue, 44
Smoked salmon spread, 18
Smoky seasoning, for nuts and seeds, 67
Snails on toast, 48
Snails with herb butter, 48
Sour cream and Roquefort dip, 12
Sour cream mold, 20
Spicy clam spread, 18
Spicy cocktail sausage balls, 43
Spicy cocktail wieners, 43
Spicy-mint grilled prawns, 46
Spinach squares, 62
Spinach-wrapped chicken with oriental dip, 65
Spreads, 17–23
Spring rolls, 54
Square sandwiches, 63
Stuffed cherry tomato halves, 59
Stuffed clams, 77
Stuffed gouda cheese, 23
Swedish salmon appetizer, 64
Sweet and sour sauce, 55
Swiss fondue, 27

T

Tamale tempters, 45
Tartare rounds, beef, 65
Tart hollandaise sauce, 61
Tarts, cheddar, 30
Teleme or breakfast cheese with salted nuts, 22
Teriyaki sauce, 25
Thai chile sauce, 10
Tofu teriyaki appetizers, 52
Tofu tuna puffs, 48
Tomatoes, cherry, 59, 77
Tortillas, fried, 15
Tostadas de harina, 42
Triangular sandwiches, 63
Tuna, 17, 48, 61
Tuna balls with cheese dip, 48
Turkey dinner, cold, 70–71
Turnovers, 34, 35, 38

V

Vegetable-based dips, 13
Vegetable morsels, 52
Vegetables, 66
    artichoke, 39, 41, 59, 61, 77
    avocado, 11, 20
    bagna cauda, 14
    carrots, 58
    cauliflower, 58
    eggplant, 13, 17, 77
    green beans, 58
    falafil, 51
    jícama, 62
    mushrooms, 14, 38, 39, 58
    olives, 41, 58, 77
    onions, 12, 26
    parsley, 62
    popcorn, 55
    tomatoes, 59, 77

W

Water chestnuts, 17, 43
Wieners, spicy cocktail, 43
Wine, 74–75
Wine and food tasting party, 78
Won ton, Chinese, 54

Y

Yogurt sauce, 55

Z

Zippy clam dip, 10
Zucchini dip, 13

Pastry Crab Puff dipped in guacamole (page 47).